GRIEVING the DEATH of a FRIEND

GRIEVING
THE DEATH OF
A FRIEND

HAROLD IVAN SMITH

Augsburg
MINNEAPOLIS

DEDICATION

Grieving the Death of a Friend is lovingly dedicated to my friends who have waded the wide river and now reside in the far country. Each one made a distinct contribution to my life and remains part of the fabric of my life:

Denny Apple
Bob Benson
Hudson Butler
Alice Cobb
Tommy Cook
John M. Culver
Leon Doane
Billy "Rusty" Esposito
Anne Hargrove
Lois Hicks

Martin Alan King
M. E. Bud Lunn
Fred Z. Marty
Donnie Mesarosh
David Messenger
John L. Moore
Bunny Oney
Cecil Paul
Martha Shedd

*I have realized I will now be less afraid to die because
you have done it first. Whatever is ahead will seem more hospitable
to me because I will think of you as being there to welcome me in
—in one more act of hospitality of the sort you have
offered me all your life.*

—Susan Ford Wiltshire [1]

GRIEVING THE DEATH OF A FRIEND

Scripture verses are taken from the Holy Bible, New International Version, copyright © 1973, 1978, 1984 by International Bible Society. Used by permission of Zondervan Publishing House. All rights reserved.

The "NIV" and "New International Version" trademarks are registered in the United States Patent and Trademark Office by International Bible Society. Use of either trademark requires the permission of International Bible Society.

Cover photo courtesy of Image Club Graphics, Inc.
Cover design by Marti Naughton
Text design by James Satter

Library of Congress Cataloging-in-Publication Data

Smith, Harold Ivan, 1947-
    Grieving the death of a friend / Harold Ivan Smith.
        p.   cm.
    Includes bibliographical references.
    ISBN 0-8066-2842-1 (alk. paper)
    1. Bereavement—Psychological aspects.   2. Bereavement—Religious aspects—Christianity.   3. Grief.   4. Grief—Religious aspects—Christianity.
5. Loss (Psychology) I. Title.
BF575.G7S59   1996
155.9'37—dc20   96-839
                                                                              CIP

The paper used in this publication meets the minimum requirements of American National Standard for Information Sciences—Permanence of Paper for Printed Library Materials, ANSI Z329.48-1984.   ∞

Manufactured in the U.S.A.   AF 9-2842

00   99   98   97   96   1   3   4   5   6   7   8   9   10

CONTENTS

PREFACE

I've struggled in writing about the death of friends, both in my doctoral dissertation and in this book. Maybe I'm making a mountain out of a molehill. Perhaps friends are to be mere blips on our emotional radar screens and "Nice to know you" is sufficient. My heart reads that sentence and says, "No way!" My friends' deaths and my responses to them have taken me back to my travels in Austria when, weary from sightseeing and wanting only a quick meal before calling it a day, I could not make my wishes known to the waiter—either in German or English or "travelerese." I tried so hard to make my hunger known, but somehow all that got lost. Finally I went to bed hungry:

I again feel that frustration.
After all, I am again a traveler,
wandering through a landscape for which Fodor
has no guidebook—a land called Grief.

Experiencing my friends' deaths has depleted my heart.
My heart lies, collapsed, like a party balloon
the morning after the celebration.
No one understands my grief.
I guess that's what I get for taking friendship so seriously.

For some time, I have told myself, "My grief counts." In this book, I want to go one step further and say to you, "Your grief counts!" And I want us, in turn, to say this to strangers who possess unresolved, unprocessed, raw, jagged-edged grief for departed friends. Grieeevve!!! Why? Because no one encourages you, as a friend, to grieve. Because you may have been halfway across the country when your friend died, you did not get to participate in the rituals. Because your employer probably had no provisions in personnel policies allowing you to attend rituals for friends. Because no one sent you a "thinking of you" card or telephoned with a word of encouragement. Because no one recognized or recognizes your lingering, unshakable grief. Because you have grieved or are now grieving alone.

9

What gives me any expertise? Really, only first-hand experience as a grieving friend. The decision to write this book came in a hotel room the night of the memorial service for my friend Rusty. I had been unable to rearrange a speaking commitment in order to attend. So, that night, I put on my emotional armor, reminded myself that "the show must go on," and spoke to 200 people, autographed books, then begged out of a late dinner invitation from my hosts.

I returned to my hotel room and sat alone in the dark, mourning and remembering. And crying. I fell asleep castigating myself for not going to the memorial service and wishing I had something that would help me process—no, learn from—this loss. After all, I'm now at that point in mid-life where there will be more deaths to deal with; where friends, like Cecil, a college president in Boston, keel over and die. Where friends like Lois die due to a surgeon's mistake and take a recipe for a fabulous carrot cake with her. I need assistance with this burdensome accumulating grief.

A second factor has motivated me. Friends who are well acquainted with their grief for their friends and my research interests have chided me, repeatedly, over cheesecake, over meals, in phone calls and letters, "When are you going to write that book? I need that book now!"

The third motivation was that many friends who read much of what I wrote in the past will not have the chance to read this book. They couldn't wait around. Their deaths have prompted me to finish this. In essence, this book is a way of honoring their contribution to my life.

—Harold Ivan Smith

THE FRIENDING

*Don't be surprised if you grieve more for a friend
than you did for a recently deceased relative. The old saying,
"You pick your friends, relatives are thrust upon you,"
holds true here. Friends are special people in our eyes
because we hold them to be. Friends fill time in
our lives that will be vacant when they die.*

—Helen Fitzgerald [1]

John L. . . . Bud . . . Cecil . . . Rusty . . . Leon . . .
Martin . . . Lois . . . Bunny . . . Anne . . . John C. . . .
David . . . Hudson . . . Alice.

*N*ames. The names of friends who have died. In a couple of instances, as a friend, I was invited to witness the dying. In some of that dying, I was "dealt in" as if it were a poker game. In too many cases the death was unexpected. The friends themselves couldn't believe that they left the party without saying good-bye. Their dying has left an ugly slash along the corridors of my heart. But had they not died, I could never have written this book. I write as a *friend-griever* whose heart aches when I hear Bette Midler sing "Wind Beneath My Wings," the theme song from the movie *Beaches*. "Did you ever know that you're my hero?"

So what happens when a close friend dies? Clearly the more valued the friendship, the more likely that the death precipitated a crisis for you, the surviving friend. To whom did you, the friend-griever, turn? Was your particular grief recognized, discounted, challenged, or ignored?

This book will encourage you to recognize your grief and to honor the death of your friend or friends, particularly if your grief was not appreciated by the family of the friend or your own family. By reading this book and reflecting, you may move closer to reconciliation with the death. Never forget: Your grief for your friend counts! Consider this lament for a friend killed by a drunken driver:

*S*eemingly everyone else,
everyone in our social circle,
has gotten over her death,
and have gone back to business as usual
while I am bogged down
in thick mud-like grief.

It's just too easy, having done the
etiquettely correct funeral things
to pretend that I am not diminished
by Barbara's death.

I am devastated!
All the platitudes we offered each other
during the initial days of shocked loss
have failed to lastingly comfort me.
I sit in my living room
and stare into the darkness
looking for some sliver of meaning in her death.
One minute Barb was here
two hours later, dead.
Thanks to a drunken driver
my friend Barb is a statistic.

I don't want Barb absent from my life
even if the pious are accurate
and she is, by their cliché,
"in a better world."
'Cause my world turned gray
and has remained gray
by her absence.

At first, it was like she was only vacationing
and I expected her to walk through
my back door, any day, announcing,
"I'm back. And I brought you something!"
At first my husband was supportive.
Ed held me while I sobbed
and snarled out my demands
for some sense to all of it.
But he told me the other night:
"You've got to get on with your life . . .
our life."
And then he rolled over, away from me,
and left me to wander the dark alone.

I don't want Barb absent from my life!
I still need her.
She was my cheerleader.
Life will never be the same without Barb.

One drunken driver tore my friend from me.
Want to know what I'm wondering
at four a.m.?
If these friends of ours,
If Ed could forget Barb so quickly,
won't they forget me if . . . ?
I know the answer to that and it's not at all
comforting in the four a.m. darkness.

—Harold Ivan Smith

Two million people die each year in the United States.[2] Assuming a range of three to five close friends per death, the magnitude of the problem is enormous. Sooner or later, everyone will be touched by the death of a friend, buddy, pal, chum, or colleague who was not a relative or spouse. *Friendgrief* is complicated and made more painful because those losses occurred or will occur in an era of friendship crisis.

Americans have great difficulty initiating and nurturing friendships given the "here today, gone tomorrow" mentality that is so prevalent in our mobile culture. In an epidemic of dysfunctional families, many of us are hungry, if not desperate, for meaningful friendships. Among the young and the elderly, friendship is emerging as the valued relationship in our culture. Many people are closer to friends than to family; friends become *de facto* families. A greeting card I recently received captures the reality with a quotation by Hugh Kingsmill: "Friends are God's apology for relatives."

These days incredible numbers of people are friendless. Others have only their spouse as a friend. Little wonder that the death of a spouse can be a double whammy. This is especially true when a wife dies. Lillian Rubin contends that husbands are more likely to consider their spouses as best friends. [3] Clearly, the description "the friendless American male" is a reality for millions of men.

After childhood, some males prefer acquaintances rather than close friends because adult friendships require disclosure and vulnerability—risky notions to many males. Somewhere, lurking in the shadows, is a common male fear: homophobia. Many men have only one non-spouse friend, and if anything should happen to that individual their social network of friends is depleted. Certainly, men have acquaintances, people they work with or go bowling with, but "real friends" are rare. Four thousand years ago, a Jewish teacher observed, "pity the man who falls and has no one to help him . . ." (Ecclesiastes 4:10).

Women, on the other hand, tend to create rich social networks and have better friendship skills—evident in both making and nurturing friendships. Because of this, women are far more vulnerable in relationships. The death of a friend can have a bigger impact on women, a reality captured in the eulogy Deena Metzger gave for her long-time friend, Barbara Myeroff:

> *I have been lucky: I have had this friendship for twenty-seven years and it has been the finest work of my life. I knew it would be when I first met her and I knew it each day we met, . . . We had risked everything, everything in the fight for her life and we lost the fight for life but did not lose the friendship. On the last day, she said to me "You did not ask for this," and I recited the traditional marriage vows: "For richer, for poorer, in sickness, and in health . . ."* [4]

What does the word friend mean anyway? What does one mean by declaring that someone "is my friend"? Well, what kind of friend? Friend requires a qualifier, such as *best, good, old, close, college,* or *longtime* for another to adequately understand the true nature of the friendship. In a culture that prizes rugged individualism, why do we need friends?

> *Friends in your life are like the pillars on your porch.*
> *Sometimes they hold you up, and sometimes they lean on you.*
> *Sometimes it's just enough to know they are standing by.*
>
> —*Marcia Kaplan and David Kaplan* [5]

Casual friendships or even *pseudo-friendships*—"He can get it for me wholesale"—compete with more authentic, deeper friendships for survival. So do mere friendships of convenience. In this age of the disposable and the "use-once-and-discard," friends are often temporary emotional liaisons. If we lose a friend, we don't worry. We'll soon make another. Promises to "stay in touch" fall by the wayside in an era of continuous change and frantic busy-ness. No wonder many people caution us not to invest too much into a friendship. That way there is little to risk or grieve.

The redefining of friendship, our obsession with mobility and individualism, and the startling rise in dysfunctional families have also complicated our mourning rituals. For many people, a friend's death today packs more of a wallop than it did in the past. Twenty years ago, if a friend in Alice's social network died, she would still have had a large pool of friends. Now, at eighty-two and living in a high-rise retirement complex, Alice keenly feels (and resents) the slow shrinking of her social network. Ironically, this is a reality she shares with her thirty-four-year-old gay grandson, although they do not talk about his losses when he visits. Both are acquainted with the grief of multiple losses and wonder who will be next. One older adult captured the grief she knows in these words:

> *As the number has shrunk, as the gaping holes multiply—*
> *as pieces of me go with those who leave this earth—I become more*
> *aware of my own mortality and the incredible sadness that*
> *endings bring.*
>
> *—Lauren Bacall* [6]

Grieving becomes clouded if your friend has been "socially devalued" by society. If your friend was mentally ill, physically disabled, HIV-positive, homeless, old, a criminal, or was an alcoholic or a substance abuser, our society can subtlety imply that this individual did not count and we shouldn't grieve. How often we offer the grieving elderly platitudes: "She lived a long life . . ." sounds to the griever like "Everybody's got to go sometime." Even people of faith dispense pre-cued "spiritual" tinted clichés: "She's with the Lord . . ." or "He's in a better place . . ." or "It was for the best."

What happens to the griever when a friend dies? Historically, the surviving friend was a passive fixture in the funeral rituals, perhaps the recipient of some brief mention in the eulogy. Male friends served as pallbearers. Today, body-absent rituals have eliminated that recognition. However, the friend is expected to attend the rituals, send a sympathy card and flowers, telephone a few times, and promise assistance with a generic, "Call me if you need anything." Societal norms make clear that a friend's grief must not compete with, overshadow, or complicate the grief of the deceased's family. Fred Sklar who has extensively studied this phenomenon concluded the following:

> *Grief is a family affair, at least in American society. The distraught close friend of someone who dies has virtually no legitimate, public grief and mourning channels. The close friend is likely to be ignored by the deceased's immediate and extended family and by others. In fact, grieving close friends may not even recognize their emotional reactions for what they are.* [7]

Sklar contends there is no "label" for the social recognition of a friend's grief. Think about these two terms: *friendgrief* or *survivorfriend*. Ever heard either as the topic for a talk show? Ever seen either phrase on the cover of a magazine in a grocery store checkout line? Probably not, because society imposes the belief that only families grieve and forces friends to submerge their sorrow, deny the validity of their emotions, forego significant public display, and watch as family members, most of whom are neither socially or emotionally close to the deceased, are granted opportunities that friends are not.

On May 18, 1995, sociologist Alice Cobb died. For twenty-two years Alice had taught at my alma mater, Scarritt College. Alice was first my professor and soon my friend. Her brief obituary stated there were no "immediate survivors." Some of her friends took offense to that statement. Alice had many survivors—friends and former students the world over. Now read this friend-friendly obituary that appeared in the alumni newsletter:

The memorial service for Alice, held at Edgehill United Methodist Church, was a celebration—a potpourri of tears and laughter as friends shared stories about Alice and expressed gratitude for her life and friendship. [8]

Try verbalizing to the deceased's family that your grief as a friend is as real and is as legitimate as theirs. "Sure." Ask the political candidate who buried seven friends in the first four months of his campaign if his friendgrief was recognized. Ask the President of the United States, whose friend committed suicide, who had to endure talk show hosts-turned-fictionists and politicians "spinning" the death into a conspiratorial murder. Ask an elder who told me, "I spent a lot of my time, these days, going to funerals."

In an era of pragmatic, discount definitions of friendship, such as, "What can you do for me?", we have *kinda-friends*. So we may mourn for what we had hoped would develop, the friendship that in time might have been. Some people are rather generous in using the label, "friend." Mary-Ellen Siegel insists that a friendship need not be of inner-circle level in order to be grieved:

Even a friendship that is not intense—one that is based on some friendly backslapping or a walk to the corner newsstand— can be experienced as an intense loss to someone to whom the interaction offered a stable routine or a recognition of self. [9]

No wonder so many people are rocked by the death of an entertainer, politician, or sports figure. Celebrities fill in the empty friendship slots in many hearts; some become fantasy friendships. For some, the death of a long-term friend can be overwhelming. This is especially true if the loss comes on the heels of the death of a family member or if it is the first first-person encounter with death. My friend Molly Porter faced this a few weeks after the death of her mother, when her longtime friend, Mike Coburn, was killed in an accident at Christmastime. Molly wrote:

My grief is so heavy over our dear friend's death—I've never had the experience of losing such a longtime and close friend—it's awful—and right on top of losing mother. [10]

Early one summer morning, after coming to the realization that my friend John was dying, I stumbled across wonderful "reminding" words from Amy Dean:

> *Each of the friends in your life—including the ones who are no longer your friends—have played an important role in helping you become who you are today. That's because every day you're on a journey in your life, and much of what you have to learn is from those you have gathered around you. Each of your friends is a valued teacher.* [11]

We're all novices in this vacuum called grief; but valued teachers are out there who can offer encouragement from their experiences. That's why you will read from a wide, diverse group of grievers who have influenced my friendgrief.

The British initially assumed the European conflict that escalated into World War I to be a mere skirmish that would be concluded by Christmas 1914. The crème of Britain suited up to go "settle" this dispute on the continent. Soon, however, Britain was hit with staggering losses, but out of that great sorrow came great poetry. This poetry was first published in newspapers because grievers could not wait for books to be published. Often the poetry appeared beside the casualty lists. Poems like "For the Fallen," which appeared in *The Times of London* on September 21, 1914, were clipped and folded, and read and reread long after the war ended. From hamlet cottages to London flats to castles in the highlands, friends grieved. One merely has to go to Cambridge and study the memorial wall of names to sense the impact of that war. A whole cohort of young friends was wiped out, and as a result many surviving friends wandered in a friendship desert for most of their adult lives.

Eighty-one years after the publication of those war poems, I stumbled across a book on the war poets. My heart trembled as I whispered the words of poet Laurence Binyon and realized that what this grieving friend had said of his friends could be said about my friends, too. "They shall grow not old, as we that are left grow old":

> *Age shall not weary them, nor the years condemn.*
> *At the going down of the sun and in the morning*
> *We will remember them.*
>
> —*Laurence Binyon* [12]

For a moment that spring afternoon, my heart beat in the rhythm of another who also knew what it was to mourn a friend's death. That's what I hope will happen as you read *Grieving the Death of a Friend*: that you, too, will remember and, perhaps, wonder why in a language as rich as ours we have only the words *widow* and *widower* when so many of us are grieving without the benefit of a socially recognized label? What about creating some terms: How about *friender*—one who grieves the significant loss of a friend?

That term describes you. That term describes me. I have come to appreciate a story about the friendship of Jonathan (son of Saul, the first King of Israel) and David (the shepherd who eventually became the second king). On several occasions, King Saul attempted to kill David. Torn between loyalty to his father and his friendship with David, Jonathan initially denied his father's actions. But when David fled into the desert for his life, Jonathan went out to his friend "and helped him find strength in God" (1 Samuel 23:16). What a paradox: the son of the man trying to kill David was the one who comforted him!

The two friends assumed that their friendship would continue after Saul's death and into David's kingship. Alas, as stories go, it was not to be. Jonathan, two of his brothers, and King Saul died in a horrendous battle. When David heard of the death of his friend, he wept and refused to eat. Eventually, through great pain, he composed a lament that he ordered be taught to the men of his army:

Your glory, O Israel, lies slain on your heights.
How the mighty have fallen! . . .

Saul and Jonathan—
in life they were loved and gracious,
and in death they were not parted.
They were swifter than eagles,
they were stronger than lions. . . .

"How the mighty have fallen in battle!
Jonathan lies slain on your heights.
I grieve for you, Jonathan my brother;
you were very dear to me.
Your love was wonderful,
more wonderful than that of women.

"How the mighty have fallen! . . ."

—2 Samuel 1:19, 23, 25-27

This lament has survived for 4,000 years as testimony to the friendship of two men and as a hint of the potential depth of friendship. Who has helped you find strength in your grief? Today, our friendgrief is often hampered, especially for men, by our inability to find words to capture it. It is so much easier for women to say, "I loved a friend." No wonder men experience such inhibited grief when a friend dies. Their mind-set limited the potential of the friendship while the friend was alive; now that same mind-set actively restricts the parameters of the grieving. The best encouragement of our grief-denying culture is "Get a hold of yourself!" or "Take it like a man."

The story of David and Jonathan challenges our casual friendships that leave us malnourished! When I read this story of friendship, I so wished for a notation that someone had gone to the grieving king and had "helped him find strength." That phrase has become one of my definitions of friend: one who helps us find strength. That's what *Grieving the Death of a Friend* will encourage you to do—to open yourself to experiencing fully the grief and to be open to the strength that another friend who is well-acquainted with grief can provide. I hope you will embrace your grief for your dead friend.

Novelist Peter Cameron captured the essence of friendgrief when he penned these words:

> *There are things you lose you do not get back. You cannot have them, ever again, except in the smudging carbon copy of memory. There are things that seem irreconcilable that you must find a way to reconcile with. The simple passage of day dulls the sharpness of the pain, but it never wears it out: what gets washed away in time gets washed away, and then you're left with a hard cold nub of something, an unlosable souvenir.* [13]

I hope you will find the strength you need to grieve well and to grieve thoroughly. On his deathbed, Revolutionary War traitor Benedict Arnold was asked if he needed anything. "Yes," he gasped, "a friend." [14] You, as a grieving friend, now echo the words of a grieving heart-broken Jewish king, "I grieve for you; you were very dear to me . . ." It's your grief. Make the most of it.

> *For the countless people who are no longer with us we are enormously grateful. In their life they added a sparkle and a magic to our days. And in their death helped to remove the veils of our fear of the unknown.*
>
> —*Vincent Lipe* [15]

THE PASSING

*The grieving begins
the moment you hear the news,
the moment you mutter your first,
"O no!"
And there will be many "O no!" moments,
believe me. I've been there.*

—*Harold Ivan Smith*

Everything is better shared.

—*Gladiola Montana* [1]

I began my mourning that first moment
I suspected there was more to the diagnosis
than he was telling me.
I suspected something was wrong
that could not be medically "fixed."

The night he told me
I felt the "Oh no!" escape my soul,
dash across my lips
and land in the space between us.
"Say it isn't so . . ." I pleaded.

He leaned forward and dropped his face
into his hands and wept like a boy
discovering his dog, dead.
"We'll fight this!" I declared.
"We'll fight it!"
I, too, now shared the struggle.

I don't remember how long my protests gushed
but finally, exhausted, we both sat staring
into the bottoms of stained coffee mugs.

"We can get another doctor . . .
a specialist . . . get a second opinion . . ."
He terminated my rambling
with a determined "No"
whimpered in his strengthlessness
after such a fit of sobbing.
I heard no exclamation mark in his voice.
I realized the issue had already been settled
in his soul.

After a too-long silence
he spoke, pleadingly,
"I want to go to the lake and fish . . ."
"I want," he paused, "us"
and his eyes italicized the pronoun
"to make enough memories in the months ahead

—if I even have months—
to stock the barrel with lots of memories
so that you won't forget me."
"'Forget you?" How could I ever forget you?

—Harold Ivan Smith

We sat in silence, too locked in our maleness to hold each other against the foul stench of death that had now occupied our friendship.

By the time I finally summoned my voice
the coffee mugs were cold.

I paused at his back door
turned and seized a long look at my dying friend
then walked across the kitchen and hugged him.
Neither of us could talk;
the words we wanted to offer
languished deep within our chests
but I am sure we both appreciated
this hint of tenderness.

Finally, I pulled away.
"Pal, I'll be here . . . for you . . ."
He started to respond
but realized that any response
would be an invitation to emotional anarchy.
But he permitted the slightest trace of a smile
and gave me a thumb's up.

I stood there long enough
to memorize his smile.
Even then I knew
I would need to remember it.

I'm not sure how long I sat crying
in my truck in his driveway.

He knew I was there
lamenting his inevitable loss.
Eventually, the porch light went off
and the kitchen went dark.

I would not know until later
how long he had stood there
peering out through the darkness at his friend
knowing he could not stop my tears.

When we became friends
we opened ourselves up to this possibility.

—*Harold Ivan Smith*

Next to the encounter of death in our own bodies,
the most sensible calamity to an honest man is the death of a friend;
and we are not in truth without some generous instances of those
who have preferred a friend's life before their own.

—*Seneca* [2]

Together we can create that place where our dying friends
can feel safe and can gradually let go and make the passage
knowing that they are loved.

—*Henri Nouwen* [3]

Hospital personnel may be slow to acknowledge the grieving friend or friends:

> *From the moment of hospitalization on, the hospital and physician gear themselves, if at all, toward the statement on the chart that reads "next of kin." Rarely are even these kin told of impending death much less are friends notified.*
>
> —*Jeannette R. Folta and Edith S. Deck* [4]

*As a friend . . . as someone who will survive him, you will have
your feelings about your friend's illness and threatened death. Not only
are you entitled to have your own feelings, but it would be impossible
for you not to have your own feelings about what is happening. The
only important thing is for you to sort out, as far as you are able,
which feelings are your own, so that you don't confuse
them with [your friend's] feelings.*

—Robert Buckman [5]

Sleepless nights are part of the grieving season; nights we do
sleep, our anxieties may be center-stage raw materials for our
dreams. I remember being almost asleep one night, reviewing the
frantic activity of the day when it dawned on me that I had forgotten to call my friend who was dying. How could I have been so
busy that I forgot to call him? It's too late to call then. My determi-
nation to call first thing in the morning did not relieve my guilt.
So I toss-and-turned in the darkness, thoroughly berating myself
for my insensitivity.

*One of the greatest services you can do for a friend is to hear her fears
and stay close once you've listened.*

—Robert Buckman [6]

Sometimes we avoid dying friends, excusing our decision with
the words "I don't know what to say" or "I'm afraid that I will say
the wrong thing," which may mean "I am not willing to be vulnerable." Such phrases assume we are supposed to know what to say.
Go ahead, take the risk and take your cues from your friend. Listen,
then perhaps respond. A friend is more likely wounded by our
ignoring their dying than by our having said "the wrong thing."

*Primarily, no matter what, you alone cannot be all things
to your friend that he may want or need you to be during his
dying process. To repeat: No matter what, you alone
cannot be all things to your friends.*

—Nina Herrmann Donnelley [7]

There's no need for a lot of talkin' when two people understand each other.

—*Gladiola Montana* [8]

———••———

Simple acts of friendliness—such as sitting at a bedside, reading to your friend, or just being there will be graciously welcomed. Edgar Imhoff learned this in the dying of his friend Kristen:

The young woman whose hand I am holding has many admirable qualities: intelligence, wit, humor, even beauty . . . none of these attributes, nor all the wonders of medicine, will erase the fact that she is dying—nor postpone it much longer.

I sit and talk with Kristen when I can; she is good company. I tell her that yesterday, in the Coast Range, I heard a canyon wren and saw a crazy prairie falcon—that had no business being up in the mountains. She laughs and tells me again about the rare blue duck that she sighted on the Milford Track in New Zealand, during her last big trip.

We break conversation, while the nurse services the medical paraphernalia attached to her. When we resume, Kristen confides: "I had a visitor yesterday who said, "I know how you feel." Ed, I was really rude to him. I said, "You can't possibly know how it feels to be lying here dying at the age of twenty-seven!" She was crying.

I touch her face and say, "Good for you, Kris! Yes."
No one but you really knows. [9]

———••———

The most I can do for my friend is simply to be his friend.
—Henry David Thoreau [10]

When there is nothing we can do for a dying friend, we can still be with them in person. Or when distance prevents our presence, by phone or letter.

We are called to stand faithfully by those who are dying, to relieve
their suffering in all ways possible when the dying person does not forbid
us to do so. The greatest fear of those dying is abandonment by loved ones,
or care-givers. It is true that each of us enters an utterly lonely moment in
dying, a moment in which one will echo Christ's own cry, "My God, my God,
why have you forsaken me?" Yet as Christians we know that the presence
of Mary [Jesus' mother] and John [Jesus' friend] at the foot of the cross
models the behavior toward the dying we should adopt.

—*James Bresnahan* [11]

I didn't go see my friend, Anne,
until the very last.
Oh, I had good intentions:
"I need to get over to see Anne . . ."
But I found ways to postpone that journey.
I chose to call although her home was only
ten minutes, max, from mine.
I didn't want to see that brilliant woman emaciated by cancer.

Finally, ashamed of my cowardice
I went to her home where she had decided to die.
Her mother met me at the front door
and directed me to the study
turned into a dying room.
She could have said, "Well, it's about time you
showed up!" but only said,
"She's missed you." I breathed a prayer and walked in to the study
and found her reading a Tom Clancy novel!
What! A Harvard-educated Ph.D. in literature
reading fiction by Clancy.?!

Since I so wanted to be in control
I chided, "Anne, if I were dying I wouldn't be reading a 700-paged novel
that I might not finish.
I believe I'd be reading short stories or poems!"
Instantly, Anne's eyes riveted on mine
until the smile slowly filled her face.
"I've never had time for this . . ." she paused,
"type of 'literature' before."
Then she laughed that distinctive laugh of hers.

The politeness ended when I confessed,
"Oh, Anne, I don't know what to say to you.
I tried to think of something all the way over here . . ." I paused,
"But I am willing to listen
to anything you want to tell me . . ."

For thirty minutes one autumn afternoon
Anne talked. I listened.
I do not know if my visit did Anne any good
but Anne gave me a great gift:
By granting me absolution for my absence
By sharing raw-edged insights
about what it meant to be a single parent dying and
to be leaving sixteen-year-old Andrew.
I walked—no I limped—away a better friend
to the next dying friend in my life.

In Anne's honor I now visit dying friends.

   —*Harold Ivan Smith*

No one should have to experience that journey alone, without help.

   —*an unidentified patient* [12]

Some people by their commitment to justice dance with premature death. On April 4, 1968, Martin Luther King Jr. was shot in front of his closest friends and associates: Ralph Abernathy, Bernard Lee, Andy Young, and Jesse Jackson. Seeing the extent of the wounding of his friend, Andy Young cried out, "Oh, God! Ralph. It's over!" Abernathy snapped, "Andy, don't you say that. He'll be all right. He'll be all right." Only Ralph Abernathy was allowed to ride in the ambulance with the dying civil rights leader. He refused to leave his friend Martin's side despite requests from physicians. Finally, one physician sadly spoke: "He's going. If you'd like to have a few last moments with him, you can have them now."

Their shared history of the marches, rallies, indignities, and threats brought two friends to this last moment in a Tennessee emergency room. But Martin Luther King Jr. did not die alone:

I walked over with Bernard to where he was lying, his breathing nothing more than prolonged shudders. Somehow I knew they would be taking his body soon as he was gone, so the first thing I did was to remove the things from his pockets and put them in my own. Then, as the remaining doctors and nurses stood and watched, I took him in my arms and held him. The breaths came farther and farther apart. Then, a pause came that lengthened until I knew it would never end. I turned to one of the nurses. "What will they do with him now?"

"First, they'll take him to the morgue."

I nodded, laid his head back down on the blood-soaked pillow, and walked out the door and down the hall to the waiting room. The others were there—Andy, Jesse, Hosea, Jones, Bevel. I told them he was dead.

But despite the deep shock, someone had to be in charge. That responsibility fell on the shoulders of his friend, Ralph:

We were all in deep shock, but somehow, someone—perhaps Jesse— told me that Coretta [Martin's wife] and Juanita [Martin's daughter] were on their way from Atlanta; it occurred to me that they would not know he had died. If they had to learn the truth at the airport, I wanted to be there to tell them rather than have them hear it from some reporter. I turned to Solomon Jones, "How about taking me to the airport?"

—Ralph David Abernathy [13]

The death of a friend becomes a mirror in which we peek at our own mortality—a thought we would rather avoid:

Death is stalking me. I know because I can't see as well as I did last year. I don't last as long in my exercise class as I did last year. I can see death casting its shadow over my body. . . . It is frightening to realize, however, that I'm becoming that age when I increasingly find myself walking friends and loved ones through sickness and disease, and bidding some farewell in death. I cannot write myself out of death's hold on us. I don't know what the future holds. So I spend my days making the best choices I can about how to live out the days I have allotted. I do not ask God for more time. Instead, I ask for what the elders call "a reasonable portion of health and strength." More importantly, I do not ask for riches. Rather, I ask for people in my life who will love me enough to comb my hair and wipe my mouth should the days come when I am no longer able to do either for myself. For my remaining days, I ask for intimacy.

—Renita J. Weems [14]

Sometimes friends walk the death path simultaneously, as did two signers of the Declaration of Independence. In July 1826—on the eve of the fiftieth anniversary of the signing, two patriots lay dying hundreds of miles apart. The correspondence between John Adams, the nation's second president, and Thomas Jefferson, the third president, indicates that death had been a subject of speculation between them. When Abigail Adams died, Thomas Jefferson (a widower) wrote the following to John Adams:

I know well, and feel what you have lost, what you have suffered, are suffering, and what you have to endure.

Although Jefferson had reservations about eternal life, he comforted his grieving friend Adams by saying that in the "not very distant time both of us" will join "an enthusiastic meeting with the friends we have loved and lost and whom we shall still love and never lose again."

These words, seldom cited, in essence compose a declaration of independence from the tyranny of death. Just before midnight on July 3, Jefferson asked a friend at his bedside, "This is the Fourth?" "Almost" the friend replied, fearful that Jefferson would not last until sunrise.

Jefferson died believing that his friend was still alive. In Massachusetts, Adams's last words were, "Thomas Jefferson survives." [15] In an era of slow communication, it took the citizens of the young nation nearly a week to discover that both friends died the same day—July 4.

There comes a time to say "good-bye." Friends at death's door have been surprised that their planned, even rehearsed, speeches often go unspoken. One of the infamous greetings in modern history was spoken by journalist Henry Stanley when, after months of searching across Africa, he finally met up with the great Scottish explorer: "Doctor Livingstone, I presume." The two men became friends and explored Africa together. Their last meeting—which both friends knew would be their last—was difficult:

We had a sad breakfast together. I could not eat, my heart was too full;
neither did my companion seem to have an appetite.

Stanley spoke to this man who had become his friend:

And now we must part—there is no help for it.
Good-bye.

But Livingstone would have the last word:

Oh, I am coming with you a little way.
I must see you off on the road.

So, the two explorers walked their last trail together, their servants softly singing, Stanley taking "long looks on Livingstone, to impress his features thoroughly on my memory." Stanley's biographer captured the paradox of that last handshake.

So they parted, these two great African travelers, so incongruously different in character and in their life's purposes—the one to a death in the jungle swamps of Bangweolo, the other to fame, fortune, and the founding of the Congo State (now Zaire). [16]

In essence, as a friend, like Livingstone, we can accompany the dying "a little way." We, too, can see our friend "off on the road" called dying.

Sometimes issues must be resolved for the friend to die and for the friend to survive in peace. A rift had developed between George Washington and Henry Knox, a member of his Cabinet. Finally, in 1799, Washington reached out to his estranged friend with a friendly letter. On December 22, Knox wrote back the following:

> *I may not wish you the greatest blessing by wishing you a long life, because I believe that while you continue here, you are detained a much better condition. But I pray fervently that your days on earth may be days of felicity, without clouds, sickness, and sorrow.* [17]

Because it took a longer time to deliver mail in those days, Knox did not know that the general had died a week before Knox wrote the letter. In an era of telephones, fax machines, and jet travel, it is difficult to imagine that many throughout history only learned of a friend's death long after the passing. Most people were denied the opportunity to be with a friend before death or to participate in the rituals.

In the hotly contested 1968 presidential election, Republican Richard Nixon defeated Democratic vice-president Hubert Humphrey by 510,000 votes (out of 72 million cast). Commentators suggested that if Humphrey, who was moving up in the polls, had distanced himself from the highly unpopular Lyndon Johnson, he would have been elected instead of Nixon.

Ten years later, Nixon was living in San Clemente and forced to resign as president in 1974. Humphrey, again in the Senate, was dying of cancer. Senator Humphrey decided it was time to "mend some political fences." On January 9, 1978, Nixon's birthday, Humphrey called with birthday greetings. For fifteen minutes, the two former adversaries talked. Nixon agonized with his estranged friend's pain. When the conversation ended, Nixon told an aide, "He's only got a few days. I don't care what it takes, but I'm going to his funeral. Start working on it." Two days later, the vice-president died, and widow Muriel Humphrey said she would be "honored" to have Nixon attend the services.

Stephen Ambrose, Nixon's biographer, described the former president as "gloomy and depressed, whether by Humphrey's death or his return to Washington, or both." He wanted to cancel a pre-funeral gathering of dignitaries in the Capitol office arranged by Senate minority leader Howard Baker, but Baker insisted he come. When Nixon arrived, he found President Jimmy Carter, former president Gerald Ford and Betty Ford, former vice-president Nelson Rockefeller, and Henry Kissinger. "It was," Ambrose noted, "an awkward moment" until Ford walked over, offered his hand, and said, "Good to see you, Mr. President." They chatted about golf scores, then the others came over. [18]

Deaths and funerals can offer lots of "awkward moments." The approach of death had healed the breech between Humphrey and Nixon and started Nixon on a path to public restoration, fully experienced when Nixon died in 1994.

Some friends fear losing emotional control in front of the dying friend. "I almost lost it" or "broke down" we confess later, as if that control is a virtue to be prized. When there have been many deaths, the mourning gets stacked like firewood. Reverend Michael Piazza, pastor of the Cathedral of Hope in Dallas, has lost many friends, each death ricocheting across the canyons of last. Piazza's grief work never gets "finished"; the griefs overlap.

> *I have buried hundreds of young men in the prime of their lives, many of whom were my friends, all of whom were my brothers. I have wept and cursed and laughed with them. I have walked out of their hospital rooms and slammed my fist against the elevator wall in almost every hospital in Atlanta, Jacksonville, and Dallas. There have been hundreds of times when I have said: "I can't take this anymore."*
>
> —*Michael Piazza* [19]

Sometimes family members, anxious to protect the dying, discourage friends from visiting. Adlai Stevenson had been a close friend and political ally of Eleanor Roosevelt, who had orchestrated Stevenson's 1952 and 1956 campaigns for President. Yet, as Eleanor Roosevelt was dying in 1962, Stevenson, ambassador to the United Nations, was turned away at the hospital, a crushing humiliation. "But I am her friend," he protested. Stevenson was told that Eleanor Roosevelt did not want to be seen "in her invalid condition." Still, the ambassador persisted; he wanted some opportunity to say good-bye. Finally, in desperation, he sent a note to her:

Dearest Eleanor:

> *I have been getting regular bulletins from Maureen and pray it won't be long before I can come to see you—and what a long deferred visit it will be! . . . I love you dearly—and so does the whole world! But they can't all come to see you and perhaps I can when David Gurewitsch [her physician] gives me permission.*
>
> *Devotedly—Adlai* [20]

The family, realizing that Stevenson had been "deeply hurt" by the rebuff, decided that he would be allowed "to stand at the door and wave to her." "Come, if you would like," daughter Anna Roosevelt said, "but I don't think she will recognize you." How could she from that distance? Stevenson, accepted the invitation on the family's terms, "dropped everything and came" not to the bedside, but the doorway of his dying friend. [21]

Your partings may be just as awkward when the family is in a control mode:

*That nurse said it was "irregular" since I wasn't "family," but she
let me slip in for in her words "just a few minutes."*

*That nurse apparently was not used to stretching hospital visiting
policies to accommodate the wishes of "mere" friends.*

*It's amazing: You can hate someone and yet if you are biological
family get in to see them even if they don't want to see you!*

*In that dark room I found what was left of my once-healthy friend all
tubed-up, hooked-up, machines whirring and blinking.
I felt my heart go to pieces.
They call this humane care?*

*All the way across town, in traffic,
I had rehearsed my hope
that she would be awake
or would awaken at my voice
and grin, or squeeze my hand,
and perhaps call my name.
Although the family had told everyone:
"No visitors!" "Only family!"
I had to see her.
Luckily, for me, and I think for my friend,
the family had gone down to the cafeteria.
Every moment counted.*

*I was immediately disappointed;
My fantasies had been wasted.
Marilyn was deep in the dying.
Yet, I remembered some television show.
In a similar situation an actor,
whose name I have forgotten,
just talked to the body in the bed,
over and over saying, "I know you can hear me."
So, that's what I said to Marilyn,
"I know you can hear me.
I can't stay long."*

With eyes darting to the door,
I told her what I wanted to say:
What a wonderful friend she had been to me,
The best friend I had ever had
And would ever have.
I told her I hoped when it would be my time
to wade the wide river,
that she would come, stand on the other side
and wave me across.
I sobbed away the rest of my time.
Finally, I leaned forward
and kissed her forehead.
I had said my piece and found my peace.
I had said goodbye to my friend.
I went away quite certain that she had heard me.
Marilyn always was a good listener.

—*Harold Ivan Smith*

Death sometimes comes in pairs. Nelson Mandela, soon after his release from 28 years in prison, grieved when his friend Chris Hani was assassinated by a militant right-winger opposed to the coming political change in South Africa. Mandela grieved doubly because he knew he would need Hani's help for a peaceful transition of power. Then, two weeks later, death called again. He said that while the death of Oliver Tambo "did not shake the nation, . . . it shook me." Tambo's stroke, without warning, sent Mandela rushing to his friend's side, but he arrived too late. "I did not have a chance to say a proper good-bye, for he was already gone."

Though we had been apart for all the years that I was in prison,
Oliver was never far from my thoughts. In many ways, even though
we were separated, I kept up a lifelong conversation with him in my
head. Perhaps that is why I felt so bereft when he died. I felt, as I told
one colleague, like the loneliest man in the world. It was as though
he had been snatched from me just as we had finally been reunited.

—*Nelson Mandela* [22]

As Mandela and others have discovered, death has a way of slipping into our secure worlds and stunning us through heart attacks, accidents, murders, and suicides. Have you ever said, "Dead? No, that's impossible. I ate lunch with her yesterday." Or "He seemed so much better last night." Dean Dwyer, a twenty-six-year-old husband and father of a seven-week-old baby entered the intensive care unit at the Queen's Medical Center in Honolulu determined to fight his cancer; he wanted to see his son grow up. He chose Jeannie M. Hittle to be his "primary" nurse. Jeannie—just like some of us—received the news of Dean's death on her home answering machine:

I raced to the hospital to see Dean's family and give my condolences. They were very grateful for everyone's care. We exchanged many hugs. Dean's wife handed me their baby to hold. Tears ran down my face.

Dean's death affected me profoundly. His death somehow seemed less believable and touched me more personally than others, perhaps because I was able to speak with him and get to know him . . . I allowed myself to relate to Dean and his family as people, not as a diagnosis.

I feel guilty, angry, and bewildered. Dean's death triggered feelings like those I experienced as a child when people in my family died. In my heart I kept feeling that he was too young to die.

I was angry at Dean for ignoring the growth on his testicles. I was angry at my fellow clinicians. Why is it, I thought, that we can keep a 90-year-old alive but we couldn't stop Dean's lungs from hemorrhaging?

—Jeannie M. Hittle [23]

I appreciated the nurses, like Jeannie, who so faithfully cared for my father; in his repeated hospitalizations, they became his friends, friends he loved to tease. I was touched that two attended his funeral. Nurses grieve, too, when patient-friends die.

We live in a violent culture. The "unthinkable" can happen seemingly without warning, sometimes to friends who happen to be in the wrong place at the wrong time:

On this day a year ago, while visiting my parents, I awoke after a fitful night to the sounds of my father's sobs. He stood in the hallway, holding the morning paper. My father told me that a troubled man whom I love and have prayed for for years, had been arrested for the recent murder of a devout woman I knew and respected. . . . I'd spent hours alone with him. Did he do it? Could it have been me? Why hadn't I feared him? Should I?

Initially, My fear was paralyzing. For the remainder of my vacation, I slept upstairs near my mother—I hadn't done that in more than 20 years.

Yet I was truly terrified.

After living with fear for several months, I decided I must face it head-on. What was I afraid of? I honestly admitted my fear of intrusion and violence—the unknown things I cannot control. I fear for my infant daughter's well-being. I do my best to ensure my safety and hers, because, deep down, I guess I doubt that God will protect us. In fact, I know that God didn't keep safe my friend who was murdered.

—Rebecca Laird [24]

Visiting a dying friend can be logistically as well as emotionally difficult, especially when the friend lives some distance away and opportunities to visit are limited. Doris Grumbach, nearly eighty, was determined to go say final words to her dying friend in New York:

Feeling older than ever, I board a train at seven in the morning, a shining silver bullet aimed at a straight shot up the East Coast from Washington to New York, depended upon by this aging body to get me to the Hotel Chelsea on Twenty-Third Street in time to bid my friend goodbye, to tell him how much I will miss him, how I despise the irrational fate that determined it.

Would I have said these things? I will never know. Arrived at the door of his apartment, I find he is not there. His friend, Tony Blum, tells me he died three hours ago. Bill, a man at the height of his physical and intellectual powers. A young man (to me) who understood the value of full friendship with this old writer. I rage against my own survival in the

*darkness of his disappearance. I hate being an age he will never see,
I detest his leaving before I can say farewell.* [25]

The experience can be more difficult and life impacting, when the griever is a child. Listen to thirteen-year-old Emily's experience:

> *I have never lost but one friend near my age. . . . My friend was
> Sophia Holland. . . . I visited her often in sickness & watched over her
> bed. But at length Reason fled and the physician forbid any but the
> nurse to go into her room. Then it seemed to me I should die too if
> I could not be permitted to watch over her or even to look at her face.
> At length the doctor said she must die & allowed me to look at her a
> moment through the open door. I took off my shoes and stole softly into
> the sick room. There she lay mild and beautiful as in health & her pale
> features lit up with an unearthly smile. I looked as long as friends
> would permit & when they told me I must look no longer I let them
> lead me away. I shed no tear, for my heart was too full to weep. . . .
> I told no one the cause of my grief, though it was gnawing at my very
> heart strings.* [26]

Emily's last name was Dickinson. Thus, noted her biographer Thomas H. Johnson, it is no surprise that she touched on the theme of death in more than 500 of her poems.

Dorothy Freeman had a positive encounter on her last visit with her friend, environmentalist Rachel Carson. They had kept up an incredible correspondence over a fourteen-year period. Ironically, Dorothy wrote one final letter to her friend, mailed the day Rachel died, which revealed how Dorothy valued what proved to be their last visit:

> *My waking thought is always, "How did Rachel sleep?" I can be
> sure you wake up to bird song which I enjoyed so much in my snug
> little apartment beneath you.*
>
> *Dearest, I want you to know that yesterday I realized I had come
> home with a great sense of peace about you—not about your health—
> but about the fact that at last I know you are being cared for as I have
> wanted you to be for so long—someone to be with you at night and to
> give you loving tenderness during the day.*

> *I have just now opened my desk drawer to find the letter dated Jan. 2 which you left after that visit. You called it a "precious oasis in time, to be cherished and returned to in memory always." It was just that, dear. "Four days in a quiet bower stored with peace and precious memories of all that we have shared." How wonderful that we could have them before the storms broke.* [27]

Now is the time to say good-bye, however difficult. Friends also must make and take the time:

> *I believe in taking time to say goodbye, and not putting it off until another day.*
>
> —*Ted Menten* [28]

If you have a friend worth loving,
Love him. Yes, and let him know
That you love him, ere life's evening
Tinge his brow with sunset glow.
Why should good words ne're be said
Of a friend—till he is dead?

—*Anonymous* [29]

For some friends, time spent with the dying friend can be the most precious legacy of the friendship—even when we don't know what to say:

> *When I held Rick's hand and looked into his fear-filled eyes, I felt deeply that in the short time he had still to live could be more than a brave but losing battle for survival. . . . Rick said, "My friends shall have a future. I have only death to wait for." I didn't know what to say, and I knew a lot of words wouldn't do him any good. Instead, I took his hand in mine and laid my other hand on his forehead. I looked into his tear-ful eyes and said, "Rick, don't be afraid. Don't be afraid. God is much closer to you, much closer than I am. Please trust that the time ahead of you will be the most important time of your life, not just for you, but for*

all of us whom you love and who love you." As I said these words, I felt
Rick's body relax, and a smile came through his tears. He said, "Thank
you. Thank you." Then he reached out his arms and pulled me close to
him and whispered in my ear, "I want to believe you. I really do, but it
is so hard."

—*Henri Nouwen* [30]

On occasions this may be because there isn't anything to say. So, don't
be afraid to say nothing and to just stay close. Sometimes a touch or an arm
around the patient's shoulder is of greater value than anything you say.

—*Robert Buckman* [31]

Some people have found that it helps to pray for or with the
dying friend. Chris Glasser had a friend report an encounter with an
angel, a "sighting" Glasser believed because the patient was a medical professional. Well, angels are "in" these days. Recalling that
discussion comforted Glasser as he sat with a dying friend:

I had been holding his hand for quite some time, when I decided
to pray aloud with him. It could have been my own wishful thinking,
but his hand seemed to grasp mine together as we prayed. In his semi-
conscious state, I could have appeared as an angel to him. In reality,
I was a friend reaching out to him as best as I knew how. But I hope
he chose to believe I was an angel.

—*Chris Glasser* [32]

As Doris Grumbach vacationed in Europe, she found dying
friends still on her mind. She observed this:

I spent my last day in Paris scurrying around the shops to
find last-minute, ill-considered presents for friends and children. . . .
I made one stop at the great, ugly Romanesque Madeline church.
It was vast and empty. The pew I knelt in smelled of fresh urine.

*I didn't move but stayed instead among the minor unpleasantries
to pray for Richard, who is now close to death. Amid all the lavish
display in the past two weeks, his suffering stands in clear contrast.*

*"Holy Mary, mother of God, pray for him now and at the hour
of his death."* [33]

Sometimes the dying want to give a friend a gift to remember
them by. Beatrice Ash, who has worked extensively with the dying
through hospices, suggests special gifts as well as a warm memory
of a gift given before death. How do you know the gifts will get to
the right parties? So Beatrice suggested to Dorothy, an older woman
dying with cancer, that she give her designated possessions now:

*When I suggested she give her things to her friends while she was
still living, Dorothy was hesitant. She didn't want to make people
uncomfortable. Eventually, though, she agreed to try it if the opportunity presented itself. It didn't take long before her chance came.*

*A woman from church came to visit her. Dorothy knew her well
enough to explain what she wanted to do and her hesitancy.
The woman graciously received a lovely reminder of their friendship.
Dorothy began inviting her friends over for tea and made a private,
meaningful ceremony of giving the gifts she had planned to have
her attorney distribute. In so doing, she gave a part of herself in
the form of special memories to her friends.*

—Beatrice Ash [34]

Receiving the gift can be difficult, especially before the death,
as one griever wrote:

*David was a generous person. He would frequently buy gifts
for his friends. One day David asked me to try on the new leather
jacket he was wearing. I did and he said, "Just as I thought. It looks
better on you than on me. You can have it after I die." About a
month before he died, David handed me the jacket while I was visiting. I went into my car with it and screamed and screamed.
I couldn't imagine life without him around!* [35]

Friends can model "good" grief and help the family grieve as well. As David Deyo died in 1991, he fought to remain on his own as long as he could. His friends made that wish a reality. When asked what helped her through the long painful ordeal, his mother, Virginia, answered with the following:

I have gotten so much comfort out of his friends, I can't tell you. It was just the most wonderful revelation to me when I was there after he died and I saw how supportive these young people were, and how much they cared for my boy. Of course I cared for him too, but I always felt that maybe I was prejudiced in thinking that he was such a wonderful person. But when I realized that all these other people felt the same way I did, that was the most wonderful thing to me. [36]

The family of the dying, your own family, perhaps even other friends, may not understand your grief. Not all people accept the risk of loss that is necessary to experience the deep joys of friendship. Some may not appreciate your grief for a dying friend. For too many people, losing a friend is like losing a puppy. "Not to worry! You'll get another one. Probably someone's waiting in the wings right now—some acquaintance, more than likely, just waiting for the vacancy to be announced. And with your outgoing personality there will be lots of volunteers to be your new friend." Sadly, you will have to remember this . . .

As a defense against their own feelings of impotence and pain, they may prematurely bury their friend, in order not to have to suffer with him during the course of his dying.

—*Nina Herrmann Donnelley* [37]

Life teaches us that now is the time to love: a minute, an hour or a day from now may be too late. There are many whose lives are dependent on our loving them . . .

—*Carmen L. Cartagirone* [38]

Do not save your loving speeches
For your friends till they are dead;
Do not write them on their tombstones,
Speak them rather now instead.

—*Anna Cummins* [39]

Hawley Lincoln's experience during the passing of his best friend may be helpful to those readers hesitant to get or be fully involved in a friend's passing:

Before my closest friend died last fall, he kept his illness from me because he was fearful of my reaction. Knowing him, I knew he didn't want anyone to be bothered by his problem of a terminal illness. When I learned of the illness, our relationship grew in intensity. It was probably one of the best learning experiences I could ever have had. We laughed, we cried, we complained, we reminisced, and we waited for the final CAT scan. Within two weeks, he was gone.

The quality of one's experience visiting with, discussing and arranging funerals for people one does not know is a far cry from providing for those who are close, when one is expected to keep a "stiff upper lip." However, to process the casket containing the remains of a close friend is just short of hell. [40]

My grandfather's best friend, a funeral director named Herman Gilbaugh, conducted his funeral. But Mr. Gilbaugh told me that he had stopped embalming when his own friends started dying. I noticed the tears in his eyes and the slight tremble in his voice as he said, "I just can't do that anymore."

Although your friend's death was "just short of hell" for you, too, there is the flip side. True friends . . . are no burden when you carry them—no more so than carrying yourself would be. The burden carried by a friend is yours to share, and your burden is also his, for you know your fates are linked.

—*Arnold S. Beisser* [41]

I found prayer a comfort as my friend John Culver died. John was no more of a "church person" than he had been during his adulthood. He had faith—strong faith—but oh, how much he wanted to live. He had so much more yet to do, to see . . . I belong to a congregation that has an intercessory prayer group. On Sundays communicants fill out small prayer cards naming people and situations for which they desire prayer. On Thursday mornings, a group of people gather in the choir loft and go through those cards praying for each, often praying for people they do not know.

Sunday after Sunday, I wrote on the card, "Please pray for my friend John, who is dying." I do not know who prayed for John or even how they prayed. But it was comforting for me to know that every Thursday morning someone knelt in that sacred place and repeated John's name and reminded the God who deeply loved John that he was dying. I suspect that they also prayed for me—that God would help me "lose" my friend with grace.

In those last weeks, when I knew little to say to comfort John in our phone chats, other than trivia, I reminded him that I was praying for him and that members of my church were praying for him by name.

I felt so frustrated, 1,500 miles from my dying friend. I kept sending cards and clippings. I wanted him to know that he was still in my thoughts and on my heart. I felt so helpless . . . all I could do was pray.

I finally told him that I felt helpless. That I wished there was something more I could do. "All I can do for you is pray for you . . ." One of the last things John said to me was, "Tell them to keep praying; that helps . . . I need it."

Sometimes it's difficult to be creative in prayer when our friend is passing. You might want to try using this older prayer as a starting point:

> *Help us, God, we pray in the midst of things we cannot understand, to believe the truth in the communion of saints, the forgiveness of sins, and the resurrection to the life everlasting.*

> —*The Book of Common Prayer* [42]

*Dear Lord, welcome this traveler who has roamed the whole world
with an eager and observant eye and a responsive heart.
Welcome as he/she goes forth now
on a journey to a new place.*

*Help me to accept the fact that _____ is parting from me now,
traveling far away from me, and help me to hope
that we will be rejoined some day.*

—*Joan Bel Geddes* [43]

---

*O God, my friend is dying.
You already know that
but I need to say aloud
that dreaded word: dying.
Take my friend gently into your presence.
And bring her to peace.
And bring me peace.
Be with me as I walk my particular griefpath.
Amen.*

—*Harold Ivan Smith*

THE BURYING

Once I attended memorial services; now I plan and
give them, each service smaller than the one that preceded it.
At each, grief washes over me like a wave; then time passes
and I struggle up to breathe again, but lonelier now—
another swimming companion has been left behind.

—Fenton Jones [1]

The burying ritual—notification, wake, visitation, funeral or memorial service, perhaps a celebration, burial, or scattering of ashes—is preceded by an announcement that makes the friend's death "official." That announcement is the newspaper obituary. Even if we were present just before or at the time of death, the reality may announce itself most powerfully with the crispness of a morning newspaper's pages turning, as we quickly skip ahead in search of the obituaries. Some people start the day by scanning the obituaries.

> *In recent years, as my personal friends have begun to die—as the obituaries I now scan in the Times every morning often include a man or woman I have known or admired—I have felt,with increasing ease, that now familiar feeling of loss and sorrow, and yet that comfort, acceptance,at home with death. I have lost my terror and denial of death. I can live with its reality.*
>
> *—Betty Friedan* [2]

She died. My friend died.
I read it in this morning's paper.
One hundred and fifty-six words.
I counted them.
I had nothing better to do.
Actually, sixty-eight words dealt
with the details of the funeral
and the burial.
So, that means, as a result of subtraction someone
summarized Jill's life in eighty-eight words!
All some folks will ever know of my friend
are those words.
It would take me eighty-eight words
to describe Jill's smile
and another eighty-eight
to describe her laugh
and hundreds of words
to capture her ways of friending.
Too bad you have to pay the newspaper
to print obituaries by the word.

—Harold Ivan Smith

How we learn of a friend's death and the order in which we are notified can be telling. Being the "first" or among the first to know is part of the competitive landscape of some friendships:

> *I had learned Denny's suicide as I stood in my kitchen in New York early one morning—a February morning in 1991—glancing at the* New York Times. *On the obituary page, a headline over a three or four inch story said, Roger D. Hansen, 55, professor and author. Denny? I couldn't believe it. My first thought was that there were, as we had always known, other Roger Hansens. But when I started the story, it quickly became obvious that Denny was the Roger Hansen in question.*

> *Couldn't believe it? As I read the obituary, it occurred to me— and I suppose this was a further shock—that, not having seen Denny in years, I didn't have enough facts about him to judge his suicide believable or unbelievable. Others, in kitchens, in offices, on buses and elsewhere in the city, saw the obit and called a friend to ask, "Have you heard about _____ ? "*

> *In the days that followed the item in the* Times, *there was a lot of phone calling. It soon became apparent that it had been years since any of Denny's Yale friends had spent an evening with him or sat down at a meal with him. Some of the discussion on the phone, of course, was about what had gone wrong . . .*

> —*Calvin Trillin* [3]

We live in a time when people have a lot of negative attitudes about funeral rituals. Some dismiss them as archaic! But funeral rituals have an important secondary function: they provide a formalized gathering time and place for friends as well as for family to grieve. The gatherings can become something of a reunion, especially when conversations begin, "Do you remember the time . . ."

> *It is extremely important to come together as friends, for in grief we need others, particularly if our right to grieve is being denied.*

> —*Elizabeth Stuart* [4]

Viewing the body of our friend can have the wallop of a sledge-hammer on fine crystal. Few hearts can withstand such a blow. This necessary moment punctuates the reality of our friend's death. Whether world leader or average citizen, the viewing hurts.

I'm not good to be around
at visitations
especially visitations for friends.
Those "she looks like she's sleeping"
denials of cruel reality.
I get agitated mostly over little things.
People say the stupidest
things in funeral homes,
like they leave their brains
in the parking lot.
"Oh, she's with God."
Well, I wish she were here right now
rather than "with God."
What does God need with
my friend Margaret?
I wish she were here
to go shopping with me tomorrow afternoon.
There were things I could tell Margaret
that I cannot tell anyone else.
Who will listen to me now?
We'd been through so much together
that I just assumed
we'd make it through cancer, too.
Ever since we were neighbors on 63rd Street
raising children on no money,
dreaming our big dreams
about our futures.
Futures we've shared.

I've been sitting here at this visitation wishing everyone would
stop being so nice.
I wish someone had the courage to scream,
"This is an outrage!"
I want someone to be as angry as I am
that my friend died too young.

We had a code word between us
when social "demands" got too much.
One of us would say, "Beeee nice" and
punctuate it
with the slightest hint of a smile.
OK, Margaret,
I'm being nice at the visitation
but I'm not making any promises
about the funeral.

—Harold Ivan Smith

Throughout his years in prison, South African political activist and leader Nelson Mandela kept a "long-distance" relationship with his friend Oliver Tambo. Nelson had not been out of prison long when his friend died unexpectedly. The viewing was difficult for the soon-to-be leader of South Africa, because he had so counted on having his friend's assistance in governing the new country.

I felt, as I told one colleague, like the loneliest man in the world.
It was though he had been snatched away from me just as we had
been reunited. When I looked at him in his casket, it was as if part
of myself had died.

—Nelson Mandela [5]

But not everyone gets to pay their last respects.

At the recent funeral of a friend's father I thought about George
Herbert's comment: "Life without a friend is death without a witness."
One of the speakers at the memorial made reference to the man's
remarkable penchant for friendship, yet there were few in attendance
at the service or at graveside. At 82, the man had outlived his friends.
Sometimes death without a witness is merely a measure of longevity.
But those who do live long enough to witness a friend's death want to
be allowed to be part of it.

—Lotty Cottin Pogrebin [6]

The loss of a long-time friend is challenging. Our history, our memories, are interwoven with theirs.

The joy of working a lifetime in one place is the closeness of the friends you make.

You remember one another as you were. You value one another as you have become.

The hurtful part about having such friends is that time, being savage, eventually begins to take them.

On a day not long ago, more than half the friends I've ever known gathered in a church to pay respects to one of our own. We've had such reunions too often in recent years.

The church was full, but there was seating in the balcony. From there the view was down upon a sea of heads, most of them gone gray or hairless. And as the pastor spoke his words of comfort from the pulpit, inside those heads the memories were turning—many of them, I suppose, memories like mine.

I was remembering George Burg in what was surely the happiest time in his newspaper life.

My contemporaries and I were all young reporters, in our 20s, still struggling to learn our craft. And George, in his 30s then, was the assistant city editor, the man we answered to.

He was a boss and a friend. . . .

That's how we were remembering him, in the glory years, swinging round in his chair and calling a name across the clutter of the newsroom and saying, "Get ready to go out!"

We were remembering that. And thinking how shortly ago it seemed.

Then the service ended, and we went out into the cold—all of us who have been friends so long, gray ourselves now, and all on our way to somewhere.

—*C. W. Gusewelle* [7]

*Etiquette gets strained
at these affairs.
I mean what am I supposed to say,
"Good to see you, again . . ."
Again?
Cause there are a lot of these
good-bye gatherings lately.
The only time I see some friends
is at the funerals of other friends.*

*It's too easy to slip on my mask
and head off to yet another funeral.
But I'm tired of funerals and memorials
so orchestrated to disguise the pain of the occasion.*

*I'm tired of denying my pain
and pretending that I am not diminished
by death's repeated excursions into my life.
I have no more friends to spare.*

*I'm tired of performances at the rituals
worthy of an Academy Award.
"Me? Oh, I'm fine. Just fine!"
"And you?" Of course, I must politely
return an equal amount of interest.
Suddenly, I'm caught in a polite embarrassment
and must quickly qualify my words
with, "Well, of course, except for this . . ."
What goes unsaid but not unthought
at funerals and memorials
sandpapers the delicate linings of my heart
later in the night.*

*I'm tired, very tired,
of all the dying
and all the grieving
and all the wondering
who will be tagged "it" next.*

—Harold Ivan Smith

Who's next? That had to be going through the minds of the world leaders who gathered in Jerusalem for the funeral of assassinated Israeli prime minister Yitzhak Rabin's funeral in November 1995. Who could have ever predicted—years before—the stirring words of enemy-turned-friend King Hussein of Jordan. But the world listened as the king eulogized:

> *I never thought that the moment would come like this, when I would grieve the loss of a brother, a colleague and a friend, a man, a soldier who met us on the opposite side of a divide, who we respected as he respected us. A man I came to know because I realize, as he did, that we had to cross over the divide, establish the dialogue and strive to leave also . . . a legacy that is worthy of him.*

> *And so he did. And so we became brethren friends. . . . You lived as a soldier. You died as a soldier for peace.* [8]

Whatever the format of the rituals, remember:
When a friend dies, a good friend,
it's OK to make a fuss.
A big fuss!

—Harold Ivan Smith

And that's one of the great uses of funerals surely,
to be cited when people protest that they're barbaric holdovers
from the past, that you should celebrate the life rather than the death,
and so on. Celebrate the life by all means but face up to the death
of that life. Weep all the tears you have in you because whatever may
happen next, if anything does, this has happened. Something
precious and irreplaceable has come to an end and something
in you has come to an end with it. Funerals put a period
after the sentence's last word. They close a door.
They let you get on with your life.

—Frederick Buechner [9]

It's a bad habit, I suppose.
I sit in the back at funerals
so I can count the heads.

Seems sad to me
to live a good productive life
and have so few people
show up for the funeral.
Yes I know people are busy these days,
too busy for funerals.
Besides, these days, folks can stop by
the funeral home
in route to somewhere else,
pay their respects,
mumble something,
sign the book
and be on their way,
with the briefest expenditure of time
and the briefest experience of grief.

—Harold Ivan Smith

But many people believe the rituals are an investment in our emotional and spiritual health.

As I entered Lydia's memorial services my heart was
burdened with grief and heart-ache. As I was sitting in the midst
of all the people that Lydia had touched, and as I began to listen to
their stories of being connected with her, my feelings of pain lessened.
I began to reevaluate the meaning our lives have in connection
with one another. She will leave a void in our hearts but
continue to enrich our lives forever.

—Barbara Blake [10]

Funerals are social occasions and invite reaction and commentary. George Gurley described one friend's funeral:

> *The funeral was a masterpiece of solemn simplicity. There was no chamber-of-commerce-style eulogy to distract us from the awesome finality of death. Afterward, we critiqued the event as if it had been some sort of theater performance. . . . After all, funerals are for the dead, members of another species. Our concerns were with finding a restroom and getting a bite to eat.* [11]

Calvin Trillin described this experience:

> *It has been my experience with funerals and memorial services that there has often been some grumbling in the car afterward. It must be natural for people feeling a loss to fasten on some factual error in a eulogy or some way that the setting or the order of the service was inappropriate. I remember the grumbling on the ride back to New York after the funeral of Mike Dodge—Michael J. Dodge, III—who was killed in 1982 by a hit-and-run driver while riding his bicycle. Mike had been living in Maine, where he was well known as a Down East humorist who appeared on a series of recordings about "Bert and I" and showed up, dressed in a yellow slicker, at college auditoriums to tell stories about lobstermen and farmers in a Maine accent so broad as to believe he had developed it before he ever entered the state. Mike was unlike anyone I ever knew. The High Episcopalian service in New Haven didn't leave much room to go into why that was true. There were a couple of terrific talkers on the platform, listed on the program as ministers . . . and I wasn't interested in hearing them read passages from the King James version. I wanted to hear them talk about Mike.*

But the speakers *didn't*—at least not to the extent Calvin Trillin and his grieving friends wanted or, perhaps, needed:

> *I remember someone saying in the car on the way home, "The departed could have been a stockbroker." Even as we grumbled, however, I acknowledged that Mike, who was an eccentric but not a rebel, had a*

traditionalist side that would have been horrified at anything other than
a proper Episcopalian funeral. . . . I suppose it was simply more conve-
nient to be angry at the service than at the hit-and-run driver, who had
eluded the police and would always elude us. [12]

When death has canceled or amended the plans of friends, the
funeral rituals can be even more uncomfortable:

> *My friend and professional colleague has died. He was always—*
> *first—a friend. Only two months ago we were planning that trip to*
> *Zamboanga (and it almost came off). He was to do the geology and*
> *I would do the hydrology of those coal mines the Filipinos wanted to*
> *dewater. With gun ships hovering about us to protect us from the*
> *Moros, it would indeed have been a last hurrah from two old guys*
> *like us. Now, this God-awful funeral. 'Preacher, you do not speak of*
> *the Tom Friz that I knew.' No, that one is somewhere else now with*
> *the sun on his neck and the horizon before his eyes.*
>
> *—Edgar Allen Imhoff* [13]

Some friends leave the rituals annoyed by what was either said
or what was unsaid:

> *At the recent funeral of an alcoholic friend, the eulogizer told more*
> *lies than are told at a devil's convention. Virtue my friend could nei-*
> *ther spell nor pronounce were attached to his past life by one of that*
> *new breed of clergymen, hearse chasers, who make it big by rescuing*
> *families from the shame of a nonreligious funeral.*
>
> *As we left the chapel, resentment and shame pervaded the crowd.*
> *Everyone needed to laugh out his embarrassment, but nobody could.*
> *Relatives slunk furtively away. Personally, I resented the clergyman's*
> *rudeness in forcing his narrow beliefs on the friends of a confirmed*
> *unbeliever. Friends were teased into tears when in fact they were*
> *relieved by the death of a man who had suffered too long.*
>
> *—Robert E. Kavanaugh* [14]

Sometimes it is difficult to concentrate on the formal "agenda" of the funeral. One's own grief can be interrupted witnessing the grief of others. Novelist Sallie Bingham, a member of the socially and politically prominent Bingham family of Kentucky, had two brothers die young and was struck by the grief of her brothers' friends at her brother Worth's funeral:

> *Funeral was larger and more public than Jonathan's [her first brother] had been, two years earlier. Friends from the big world were there in numbers, bright young men who were moving into positions at newspapers all over the country. They seemed very young to me as they moved about slowly in the heavy rain. They were horribly shocked that Worth had died, as though they, too, believed in immortality.*
>
> —*Sallie Bingham* [15]

Indeed, the funeral of a friend is like a large mirror in which we can observe ourselves. How many of us have quickly looked away, muttering, "My God! This could have happened to me!"

I'm sitting here at his wake now,
numb, numb all over.
There are so many people here I don't know,
obviously friends of Matt's,
friends I've never met,
people about whom he never talked.
I've never heard of them
because I've never asked.
I was never actively part of his life.
After he told me he was gay,
I said that wouldn't change things.
But it did. Didn't it?
Sure I still talked to him
but only when he called.
And I was always so eager
to fill our conversations with my stories.
I did that, of course,
so I wouldn't have to hear about his.

I never took the time
to ask him how he was
or what he did
or who his friends were.
I see all these friends of Matt's tonight
people who gave him the support
and the love that I never did.
What happened to us?
We used to be so close,
Matt and I, . . .
. . . somewhere along the line he grew up
and we stopped being friends.

—*Bill Huebsch* [16]

Losing a neighbor-friend is a double-edged loss, as Joseph R. Bankoff discovered:

We buried my neighbor Bob Strickland this week.

We celebrated seven decades of his achievements ending in several years of grace as he fought his last battle with his own body. But in that crowded church, seated among his family and friends and in the company of former presidents and leaders of Atlanta, we felt his presence—not his absence. They did not talk about his accomplishments. We knew them well. Instead, we were reminded of the encouragement that Bob Strickland gave to everyone around him. "That's a great idea!" "You're sure doing a wonderful job." "I know you can do this." "Howdy neighbor. I'm sure glad to see you."

Listening to those around me, I realized what I admired most about Bob was that he was always a cheerleader for others, not just a salesman for himself.

After they finished the simple service for Bob Strickland, they rolled his casket down the aisle. We all stood and knew that one of our best cheerleaders was passing by. [17]

Historically, when people have not known what to say at funerals, they have turned to Scripture, particularly the Psalms. Grievers have also turned to the hymnal and relied on words and music, often crafted in the midst of great, distressing grief. One of my grandfather's favorite hymns—generally classified as a "funeral" hymn—was "The Unclouded Day." To this day I can hear him singing rather confidently between puffs on his corncob pipe about his eventual reunion with his friends "over there." He sang:

O they tell me of a land far beyond the sky
O they tell me of a land far away.
O they tell me of a land where no storm clouds rise—
O they tell me of an unclouded day.

O they tell me of a home where my friends have gone,
O they tell me of a land far away
Where the tree of life in eternal bloom
Sheds its fragrance thru the unclouded day.

O the land of cloudless day!
O the land of an unclouded sky!
O they tell me of a home
Where no storm clouds rise—
O they tell me of an unclouded day!

    —J. K. Atwood [18]

Some eloquent funerals become a model of how to conduct this ritual. Sometimes famous people desire a quiet funeral; however, those plans may be altered, even set aside. Former vice-president Hubert H. Humphrey made plans for a celebration rather than a staid public funeral ceremony.

However, after his death, his plans were modified by the family and the White House. Humphrey's remains were flown to Washington for a televised service in the Capitol Rotunda. His friend and fellow Minnesotan, former vice-president Walter Mondale, delivered an eloquent and widely-quoted tribute that many people have discovered to be equally true of their friends:

He taught us how to hope and how to love, how to win and low to lose.
He taught us how to live, and, finally, he taught us how to die.

—*Walter Mondale* [19]

Presence rather than words may be more appreciated by family members of a deceased friend. Jimmy Carter, while President of the United States, worked diligently to bring peace to the Middle East and was able to forge a peace pact between Israel and Egypt. In the process, an incredible friendship developed between Carter, a Southern Baptist, and Anwar Sadat, a Moslem and the president of Egypt. When Carter was notified of the assassination attempt on his friend, he assumed Sadat had only been wounded:

Slowly, the terrible truth became known. My wonderful friend, Anwar el-Sadat was dead. Rosalyn and I sent word to his wife, Jihan, that we would come to Egypt, and we began to make plans for the trip on a commercial airliner.

However, when the White House decided Egypt was too politically unstable for either President Reagan or Vice-president Bush to attend, Carter was asked to join former presidents Ford and Nixon in composing the U.S. delegation to the funeral. Carter balked; he wanted to go as a private citizen and personal friend rather than be part of a diplomatic delegation. Eventually, his staff challenged his thinking and he agreed to accompany Ford and Nixon.

Upon arrival, after an initial visit with the new president, Hosni Mubarak, the delegation called on the Sadat family, which Carter considered "the most memorable part of those sad hours." A diplomatic snafu clearly demonstrated that Carter was a personal friend of the Sadats and not just a political acquaintance:

When we arrived at the home, Sadat's son Gamal was on the front steps to greet us. Presidents Nixon and Ford, in the car ahead of us, were welcomed first, but when the young man saw us approaching from the side, he left his post of duty, ran to embrace me, and began to weep on my shoulder. I felt as if he were my own son, and tried to console him in his grief. After a few moments we were ready to rejoin the others, who had paused for a while and then moved on into the house.

As a friend, Rosalyn Carter stayed with Jihan Sadat, since by Islamic custom only males participate in funeral rituals. Jimmy later reflected on the ceremonies:

> As I walked in the midst of kings and princes, presidents, chancellors, and prime ministers, I felt sure they were all recalling in their own fashion what Anwar and his life had meant to them.

> —*Jimmy Carter* [20]

You may not have kings, princes, or presidents as fellow mourners for your friend. Still you, too, will spend time recalling what your friend's life has meant to you. Places have real meaning for friendships, whether it is a home, office, garden, or retreat. Our minds enhance memories of friendships by including details of where important moments in the friendship occurred. Margaret Suckley was overwhelmed with memories of happier days as she entered the White House for the funeral of her friend, Franklin Delano Roosevelt:

> This is the last time I shall be at this building, in which F.D.R. has always made me feel completely at home—I want to wander in his study & look again at all his things, from the paintings on the wall to the silly little toys on his desk. Every item speaks of him & when the thought crosses one's mind that he has permanently left them in other hands, it is almost unbearable.

> —*Margaret Suckley* [21]

Friends are often asked to deliver a eulogy. For those who fear speaking in public, let alone risking losing "control" of their delicately balanced emotions, this invitation becomes a challenge: What am I going to say? What if I lose it? Just be natural. Share a story or characteristic that captures the strengths of your friend. When Kansas City Blades defenseman Mike Coleman was killed in an automobile accident in 1994, his teammate and friend Stephen Teppler was asked "to say a few words" at the funeral. Fighting back tears, Teppler chose to focus on Coleman as a friend rather than a professional hockey player:

I spent the last day with him fishing. Everyone knows Mike didn't say much, but when we fished he opened up. I hope everybody will take a piece of Mike and remember him. I will.

Another teammate, Wade Flaherty, added in his eulogy:

I'll probably think about this the rest of my life. It's something you've got to take day by day, minute by minute, hour by hour. [22]

One honor bestowed on friends is to be asked to be a pall-bearer. Once this honor was only for males, but increasingly women are serving as well. Pallbearers discover that carrying a friend to a grave can be emotionally exhausting—a tough assignment.

We rehearsed for every important
occasion in our lives—
high school and college graduations,
our weddings, best man-ing for each other.
We practiced because we believed
in tipping our hats
at etiquette. Getting it right.
But this we had never rehearsed.
All the funeral man did was
pin boutonnieres on our lapels
and march us in
to the seats reserved down front
where everyone
could stare at the backs of our heads
checking for any hints of emotion.
Then, at the end,
the moment we'd all dreaded, he said,
"Gentlemen . . ." and motioned to us.
That word ricocheted through my heart:
"Gentle men . . ."
So, the six of us gently lifted our friend
and walked stiffly toward the door and to the waiting hearse.

Again, at the cemetery, he summoned us
and again, like schoolboys, we obeyed.

The burden seemed slightly heavier
the last shuffle
and slowly we who had run and
jogged and showered and laughed
and danced and teased and
drunk and studied
reluctantly carried him
toward his final resting place.

And when we laid him down
I felt my heart shatter.
It took all the control I could muster
to put down the emotional coup
raging within me.
But I took the pain like a man.
No one would see me lose control.

∾

This is not some "feminist" thing
I realize a lot of people have done a double-take:
A woman pallbearer! A woman?
I'm tempted to snarl, "Get used to it!"
But a pallbearer is supposed to be on
good behavior.
So, I'll just say this:
I earned my place carrying this casket
in a thousand moments as his friend.
I wish this were a bad dream;
I wish my friend were still alive.
But it's a good time to smell the roses
and the roses are everywhere today.
Head up, eyes straight ahead.
Now, girl, lift!

—Harold Ivan Smith

While pallbearing, friends have been surprised by the pallet of emotions they experience. On June 8, 1968, presidential candidate Robert Kennedy was buried in Arlington National Cemetery next to his brother, John. Because the funeral ran late, a nighttime burial offered an obstacle. In the darkness, the pallbearer-friends could not find the grave site.

Soon, it became clear that the lead pallbearer, Stephen Smith, did not know where they were going; still they kept walking. Finally, Averill Harriman broke the silence, whispering:

> *"Steve, do you know where you're going?"*
>
> *"I'm not sure."*
>
> *"I have a feeling we've walked too far." [John Siegenthaler]*
>
> *"So, do I. Let's stop, and you go over and ask the man where we should be." [Steve Smith]*
>
> *"No, you go. You're the campaign manager." [John Siegenthaler]*
>
> *In that moment, Siegenthaler began laughing and soon other pallbearers were laughing.*
>
> *I could hear Bobby laughing and saying,*
>
> *"You really screwed it up—again!"*

Smith later disclosed:

> *I distinctly heard a voice coming out of the coffin saying, "Damn it, put me down and I'll go show you the way."* [23]

Sometimes a friend is too old or too ill to be an active pallbearer. Of course, one can always be designated an honorary pallbearer, but many people resent the distinction. As one man complained, "A man is in a bad way when he is too old or too fragile to be a pallbearer." Some friends are determined to be included:

I can carry my share!
I had noticed that young undertaker
eyeing me up, wondering
if I could be counted on.
What if I am the oldest pallbearer?
That's because I was his friend
the longest.
I deserve to be here.
When the mortician asked me
there was no way I could say no.
"What about your back?" my wife quipped.
"You're too old for all that lifting!"
"You'll be in bed for a week!"
"Maybe—maybe not!" I snapped.
"I'll call back and tell them you're . . ."
"The day I get too old to be a pallbearer
they can just bury me as well!"
She wasn't listening to me.
"I call them back and tell them you're not up to it . . ."
"No!"
"Why?" she demanded.
"WHY?"
"I'll tell you why. Because in 1944,
in Italy, John carried me.
To safety.
I bled all over him
like a stuffed pig
but he didn't complain.
Most of the time I was out of my mind
with pain.
But over and over he whispered to me:
"Hang on, pal, not much further . . ."
John deserved a medal but
he swore me to secrecy.
"So there. You're the first to know.

No point in keeping it secret any more.
I owe him.

The Burying

That day in '44 I heard a couple of guys
I thought were buddies yell at him,
"Leave him here!"
But my friend carried me.
So, now, all these years later,
I'll help carry him."

  —*Harold Ivan Smith*

Funeral rituals can be disturbing, or at least discomforting. One World War II veteran no longer attends graveside services. "When I hear *Taps* and see the flag being folded, I just lose it. I bawl like a baby. So I've stopped going." Others question—if not discount—the meaning of certain funeral customs, as Margaret Suckley did aboard F.D.R.'s funeral train:

> *I knew it was F.D.R.'s body that was being taken on its last jour-*
> *ney, but I also knew that F.D.R. was no longer in that body & that*
> *in all probability he was seeing this mourning procession & all us*
> *sad people from his newfound freedom, and he is wishing he could*
> *tell us not to be sad, but to tighten our armor of faith & carry on*
> *the great fight which he has been waging with such courage & faith.*
> *Perhaps his death will tie together the millions of people who were*
> *depending on him.*
>
>   —*Margaret Suckley* [24]

For some friends, the graveside rituals can be the toughest because they are so final. Some friends do not stay long; others avoid this element of the ritual.

younger
...c triumvirate of respect:
wake or visitation, funeral and burial!
Wouldn't have thought of shirking
my social responsibility
by missing any of them.
Everyone did the three rituals before we got
so frantically busy.

Now, my wife and I end it at
the church or the funeral home.
I tell people that it's because, at my age,
I don't drive so good any more.
But that's just an excuse I've crafted.

I drive better than most of my friends.

But I just don't like those
slow rides out to the cemetery
especially on cold, wet, dreary days.
It took me weeks last fall to get over
burying my friend Herb.
I got soaked in the cold rain
but it was my heart that hurt the most, afterwards.
But I do worry that when my time comes
to ride in the hearse
No one will drive behind me on my last ride.

—Harold Ivan Smith

When Barbara Boggs Sigmund, mayor of Princeton, New Jersey, died at age fifty-one, the town turned out for the seasoned politician's funeral in the Princeton University Chapel. One friend described what followed the service:

A candlelight procession through silent Princeton followed the
casket to its burial place. Then the family left, and five of Barbara's
oldest friends remained behind. We surrounded the coffin as it descended,
placed our hands upon the top and, reclaiming the hymn, "Tantum Ergo"
from our memories, we sang our old friend into the earth.

—Phyllis Theroux [25]

Now I know what it feels like to stand at an open grave
and say goodbye, to throw a handful of dirt onto a box that contains
the wasted remains of someone I loved. I now know the common sorrow
of outliving those I love. They can't be touched; yet I continue to feel them.
No more can they speak to me; yet I still hear them. Even after
they are gone, I continue to love them.

—Ronald O. Valdiserri [26]

Jesus knew what it felt like to stand at the grave of a friend, in what people initially assumed was to be a goodbye to his friend Lazarus. Indeed, John reports that Jesus was "deeply moved in spirit and troubled" (John 11:33).

Even when we knew he would raise his beloved friend Lazarus
from the dead in minutes, He wept. "Jesus wept." To you, right now,
that short sentence could be the most important verse
in the entire Bible.

—Eugenia Price [27]

If Jesus wept for a friend, I need not feel intimidated for my tears. The shortest verse in the Bible is one of the most liberating for grievers. Since Jesus cried for his friend, so can we.

———•———

When Martin Luther King Jr. was buried, the family asked Reverend Ralph Abernathy, his longtime colleague and friend, to do the committal. "By this time," Abernathy noted, "I was exhausted, as was everybody else, so I made it brief and from the heart":

> *This cemetery is too small for his spirit but we submit his body to the ground. The grave is narrow for his soul, but we commit his body to the ground. No coffin, no crypt, no stone can hold his greatness. But we submit his body to the ground.*

Abernathy later wrote of that moment:

> *At that moment I bade him a silent good-bye and turned my back on the grave, determined to make his spirit live in the army and marching orders he had left behind.*
>
> *—Ralph David Abernathy* [28]

Funerals can be difficult when the minister is also a friend, as Ron DelBene experienced when he conducted the funeral of his friend, Taylor, who had dropped dead of a heart attack at age forty-two while jogging:

> *Taylor's death consumed me with grief. I cried. I questioned. At first, I could not think beyond myself and my own pain. But then I began to feel guilty for being so self-absorbed. After all, Taylor's wife and children had lost even more than I had.*
>
> *At the funeral, Taylor's family had the support of the grieving community, which was as it should have been. But because Taylor had*

*meant so much to me, I wanted people to tell me that they were sorry
about my loss, too. I wanted to be comforted and consoled. I went
through the service and out to the cemetery feeling desolate and utterly
alone in my grief. At the graveside, one of my clergy friends came up
and put his arm around me. "You and Taylor were good friends,
weren't you?" he said.*

"Yes," I replied. "We were." That was all it took.

*With my friend holding me in his arms and offering the comfort
I needed, sobs came from the depths of my heart.*

*Losing Taylor has given me a particular empathy for others whose
best friends die. Often the family of the deceased doesn't know how
close the friendship was. Indeed, the family may not know at all.*

*Now when I preach at a funeral, I always remind myself to pay
attention to the friends of the person who has died.*

—Ron DelBene [29]

If only there were more pastors with the sensitivity of Ron DelBene.

———•———

Pastor Thomas Nelson of First Presbyterian Church in Independence, Missouri, faced a difficult graveside pastoral decision
one cold February afternoon. No one was with him except the
funeral director and the corpse. The deceased, it was assumed, had
outlived his friends so just do the ritual and go home, he thought:

*We thought we'd wait until the appointed time [as announced]
in the newspapers, in case anybody would come. . . . In came this
green Chrysler and I recognized the car immediately. I knew it was
Mr. Truman's car. The Secret Service man got out and stood in his
position and Mr. Truman walked over to the bier, and I was amazed.
I went ahead with the committal. Snow was still in the air, cold. . . .
After I had my benediction, I said, "Mr. President, why are you here?*

It's cold and it's bitter. Did you know this gentleman?" And he said, "Pastor, I never forget a friend." And I was just speechless. This was the President of the United States."

—*Thomas Nelson* [30]

Jose Tortes, former light heavyweight boxing champion, stood in the darkness at Arlington National Cemetery sadly watching the casket of his friend, Robert Kennedy, lowered into the ground:

As I looked at the casket, he [Robert Kennedy] spoke to me. I was so hurt. I had to understand what he had been trying to do. I felt it was hopeless now, that my people who had come so close to having a friend [in the White House] would never have one now.

I felt we were doomed, that nobody would help us. I heard, I swear I heard, the voice of Robert Kennedy. The voice said, "I tried. Don't despair, Jose. Things will get better. Somebody will come. I know this. Believe this." I went home and, somehow, I felt better.

—*Lester David* [31]

After the rituals have been completed, the reflection begins. Thomas Wentworth Higginson enjoyed a long friendship with poet Emily Dickinson. He wrote the following in his journal after his participation in his friend's funeral:

To Amherst for the funeral of that rare and strange creature, Emily Dickinson. The country exquisite, day perfect, and an atmosphere of its own, fine and strange, about the whole house and grounds—a more saintly and elevated "House of Usher" . . . E. D.'s face a wondrous restoration of touch . . . not a gray hair or wrinkle, and perfect peace on the beautiful brow. . . . I read a poem by Emily Bronte.

So far, just a review of the event. Higginson added a telling note that will bring a nod from readers:

> *How large a portion of the people who have most interested*
> *me have passed away.*
>
> —*Thomas Wentworth Higginson* [32]

It's amazing the teasing thoughts that dart through one's mind during funeral rituals—thoughts that may stimulate serious reflection afterward:

> *The first time a friend dies, you think: "Thank goodness it's not*
> *me." The second time you wonder: "Why not me?" And the third*
> *time you say: "When am I next?" With the others that follow you*
> *don't ask questions and more and more just hope that it [death]*
> *will pass your door.*
>
> —*"Gerald"* [33]

My friend Betty Carmack has conducted research on multiple loss and noted the inability of the griever to "finish" grieving one loss before another occurs. She says that among people who are senior adults or HIV-positive, "the sheer number of losses makes it impossible to get through the grief." One is also grieving the loss of one's entire social network:

> *This is cumulative. You can never finish with one before another*
> *happens. You can never truly fully process a loss; it's a dangerous*
> *thing, two or three or more happen and I haven't finished with the*
> *others, and they are friends.*
>
> —*unidentified griever* [34]

In many ways, we forget that the rituals are not ways to finalize a death but elements in the process of fully and publicly recognizing the loss:

> *You don't have to do all your grieving at once.*
>
> —*Marilyn E. Gootman* [35]

There is something of a paradox at work. The friend who has died may well have been the friend we previously turned to in times of crisis, in other losses:

> *Needing a friend at this time is a tribute to your friend who died. After all, your friend helped you to realize the importance of friendship.*
>
> —*Marilyn E. Gootman* [36]

Sometimes about all we can do is to offer a prayer: for the life of the departed, and for all who mourn:

> *God, welcome my friend whom I already deeply miss through the narrow gate and across the wide, deep river into your kingdom.*
> *God, in your great mercy*
> *grant [name] my friend, safe lodging,*
> *a holy rest and peace at last.*
> *Amen.*
>
> —*Jim Cotter and Harold Ivan Smith* [37]

I'm so glad they had a funeral
for Helen, after all.
Church was half-full.
At times it resumed more of a reunion.
Hugs and kisses and smiles to go around.
Helen had been like the mortar
between bricks the way
she held so many relationships together.
"And how did you meet?"
"Ah, Helen introduced us."
The eulogies were just about right.
Sometimes people "fib" a little on these occasions
but not about Helen.
I suspect she would have been
initially embarrassed
by the lavish verbal bouquets
offered in her memory.
Almost like those quilts she loved—
the eulogies were pieced together
in our hearing
while sunlight bathed mourners
deep in their private acts of remembering.
No surprises. Only reminders
of how friendship
enriches our lives.
I'm going to miss Miss Helen and her
"Oh, I have someone I want you to meet . . ."
I'm glad they had a funeral for Helen, after all.
Good to see so many I hadn't seen in years.
Good to have my memory jarred.
I'm going to miss my friend, Helen.

—Harold Ivan Smith

————◆————

*Into your hands, O merciful God, we commend your servant,
our friend.*

*Acknowledge, we humbly beseech you, a sheep of your own fold, a
lamb of your own flock, a sinner of your own redeeming. Receive
[name] into the arms of your mercy, into the blessed rest of everlasting peace, and into the glorious company of the saint in light. Amen.*

*May . . . the souls of the departed, through the mercy of God,
rest in peace. Amen.*

—The Book of Common Prayer [38]

————◆————

From the Jewish tradition comes this thoughtful prayer for a friend:

*God of compassion, grant perfect peace in Your sheltering
Presence, among the holy and the pure who shine in the brightness
of the firmament, to the soul of our dear [name] who has gone
to his/her eternal rest. God of compassion, remember all
her/his worthy deeds in the land of the living. May [name]'s soul
be bound up in the bond of everlasting life. May God
be [name]'s inheritance. May she/he rest in peace.
And let us answer: Amen.* [39]

————◆————

THE MOURNING

Now I am setting out into the unknown.
It will take me a long while to work through the grief.
There are no shortcuts; it has to be gone through.

—Madeleine L'Engle [1]

Blessed are those who mourn, for they shall be comforted.

—Jesus (Matthew 5:4)

Well just how long is all this mourning going to take? Isn't it about time I get to the comforting part? If you are going to be comforted, you will have to claim your right to mourn, particularly in a death-denying society that prefers to restrict grieving rights to the family:

> *If you have been a friend in any capacity to your . . . friend during his or her dying, know that you have done a good thing. Know, too, that you have a right to mourn; and claim that right to mourn. Don't be embarrassed or afraid to say that you are mourning your friend's death.*
>
> —*Nina Hermann Donnelley* [2]

Some people may challenge that right or question your grieving:

> *You may feel your mourning a "friend" should be limited or submerged. This is nonsense. You loved your friend. When we lose someone or something we love we have a right to mourn. And, regardless, we will mourn. After all, your friend is worth being mourned, is she not?*
>
> —*Nina Herrmann Donnelley* [3]

As a friend, you have a need and a right to grieve. Is there a particular point when mourning is initiated? Some of us would say a determined "Yes" because we so well remember that moment when an "Oh No!" erupted from deep within. For others, it was a feeling that had to be identified as mourning, perhaps by another friend who announced, "You're grieving." We had never considered grieving for a friend a possibility. In that moment, we felt the first sliver of relief. "Well, at least my pain has a name."

Our grieving is affected by when and by how we learned of either the death or the dying. In many cases, we didn't fully know or believe the prognosis, so our mourning was delayed, especially if we participated in keeping the full diagnosis from the patient. One woman in a grief gathering reported that she had ordered friends out of her husband's hospital room because they were being negative. "I thought if I could surround him with positive, loving thoughts, he would beat the cancer." Unfortunately, she lost some friends as well as a husband.

Friends commonly "compare notes": "When did you find out?" "What has the family told you?" "How did he seem to you?" "When was the last time you saw her?" Some families complicate the grief of friends by not disclosing full information about the severity of the diagnosis to friends or by denying—or at least discouraging—access to the patient, a process that the medical establishment cooperates with through "family only" codes.

In some instances, mutual comforting is negated because people want to "qualify" their relationship with the deceased friend. So "good friend" is trumped by "best friend." Even mutual friends say or hint, "Your grief doesn't count" or "My grief is greater than yours!"

Alexander Hamilton, friend of George Washington, demonstrated this reality. Washington had somewhat shielded and protected Hamilton from his political enemies but when Washington died in December 1799, Hamilton was left "on his own." Hamilton wrote Tobias Lear, Washington's private secretary and confidante:

> *Perhaps no man in this community has equal cause with myself to deplore the loss. I have been very much indebted to the kindness of the General, and he was an Aegis very essential to me.*
>
> *—Alexander Hamilton* [4]

Sometimes we suspect our pain is being weighed when someone asks, "How well or how long did you know him or her?" Marilyn E Gootman dismisses such thinking:

> *You have a right to your pain. Don't compare it to the pain of someone else who knew the person better than you. Pain is pain.* [5]

I've wondered which is a "better" death: the "didn't-know-what-hit-'em" or the long, lingering death. The latter, at least, offers some opportunities for friends to express their good-byes or to tidy-up any unfinished business.

Friendgrief can be complicated by the cause of death, particularly when there is a stigma attached, such as with AIDS, substance abuse, or suicide. Or when the death is violent and the body disfigured, so that a "closed casket" funeral is necessary. Or when the death is senseless, such as when four teens are killed after their senior prom in a car crash.

"They had their whole lives ahead of them," their grief-stricken friends protest. Mourning can be complicated for the friend who survives an accident. How well Carla Cantor knows this grief. Twenty years ago, as a teen, she and her best friend riding in a car were hit by a logging truck:

> *Twenty-two years later, I can still hear her screams. . . . They called my survival a miracle, which for the longest time I took to mean that I shouldn't have lived.*

> *Surviving a fatal accident can be a complicated blessing. There were moments when I wished I had died, the feelings of guilt were so devastating. Why hadn't I seen the turn? Why hadn't I forced Toby to wear the seat belt she said made her feel uncomfortable? Why wasn't there something I could have done to save this radiant girl?*

> *For a month afterward, every time I closed my eyes I saw the accident. I couldn't stand to drive. I never did return to high school. . . . I was too ashamed to step inside the building. Toby was dead, I was alive and didn't even have a scratch to show for the tragedy.*

> *It was as if life had started all over again with Toby's death, and the person I had been before the accident didn't exist. The guilt that pervaded my life had made it impossible for me to grow up. For me to be happy, I had to leave Toby behind, alone, forever frozen at sixteen.*

> —Carla Cantor [6]

All too frequently, grieving has been hamstrung by the widespread notion of "stages of grief," loosely based on the writings of Elisabeth Kübler-Ross. Many of her interpreters contend that mourning progresses through five stages: from denial, to anger, to bargaining, to acceptance, and finally to growth. While this concept is useful in understanding an abstract reality like grief, many counselors have suggested that the stages are always linear and will be followed through in a lock-step progression, just as second grade follows first grade. However, your grief for a friend cannot be charted or theorized. It is as distinctive as your fingerprints.

> *Here's what I learned about grief:*
> *It's not linear.*
> *It's not predictable.*
> *It's anything but smooth and self-contained.*
> *Someone did us all a grave injustice by first*
> *implying that mourning has a distinct beginning,*
> *middle and end.*
>
> —*Hope Edelman* [7]

> *Grief does not have a set schedule.*
>
> —*Carol Staudacher* [8]

Still, some people have to get out the emotional daytimer and make room for the agendas, behaviors, and moods of grief. Some will want to jockey for a more convenient moment or season. "Let's see, I can get around to dealing with this next . . ." We seek short cuts, easy answers, and quick one-two-threes to relief. Looking for a quick answer to fast forward to a "been there, done that!" may be common. But grief requires our cooperation.

Too many of us are like travelers with one intent: What's the fastest way to get to our destination? It could be getting over the death, getting on with life or, sadly, finding a new friend as a replacement.

Well, we do not "get over" our losses so easily. At best, we reconcile ourselves to the deaths. And it may require a lifetime to reach the reconciliation. Even if we have tangled with grief before, this new grief may be different.

As the widowed Eleanor Roosevelt discovered when her friend Malvina "Tommy" Thompson died, a friend's loss can be more severe than the grief for a spouse. In her widely read newspaper column, Eleanor stated that when Malvina died, "I learned for the first time what being alone was like." [9] Fortunately Eleanor had an understanding daughter who recognized her mother's grief for a friend. Anna wrote her mother:

> *My heart is here today—thinking of you & Tommy. I know it was best to have her go, after all that had happened to her; but that's no comfort when your mind & feelings are inundated . . . with thoughts and memories of what she has meant to each one of us. She was a very great person—with her unfailing interest in & understanding of others. . . . I know there is no use dwelling on how much you (& we 5, & Sus & Buzz & some of the other grandchildren) will miss her—but still not having her around is going to be hellishly hard to take.*

> *—Anna Roosevelt* [10]

Anna's phrase, "hellishly hard," is one that you possibly understand by this point in your loss. One seasoned grief counselor observed:

> *The grieving period can be delayed but it cannot be postponed indefinitely, for it will be carried on directly or indirectly. If it is not carried on directly at the time of the loss it will be done later at a much greater cost to the total personality.*

> *—Edgar N. Jackson* [11]

One of the funniest women ever on television was Gilda Radner, of the original cast of *Saturday Night Live*. One of the first people she met in New York was Alan Zweibel. Each delighted in making the other laugh. Their laughter stopped when Gilda died of breast cancer in 1989. Five years later, Alan wrote the following in his book about their friendship:

Well, I haven't mourned, and I haven't even cried yet, because even though she's dead, I just don't want her to die. I don't know why God makes people and then takes them back while they're still giving fun with the life he gave them in the first place. Just like I don't know if I am supposed to celebrate the fact that Gilda was in my life, or feel cheated that she's not here anymore. But even though her body grew to betray her, spirits don't just die. And that's what Gilda was. Even as an adult, she was still a little girl who believed in fairy tales and that if she said "Bunny Bunny" on the first day of every month, it would bring her love, laughter, and peace.

—Alan Zweibel [12]

At times, grief is like a hurricane meandering in its path but nevertheless picking up strength; eventually, it will come ashore with perhaps devastating consequences. Margot Hover's experience underscores the point that grief may act in the shadows rather than in the public eye:

Nearly five years ago, a good friend of mine died very suddenly and unexpectedly. We lived in different cities, and I suppose I had taken her so for granted that I was startled at the grief that overwhelmed me when I received word of her death. I talked to our mutual friends and contributed to the memorial rituals, and gradually, the ache of her absence subsided. I grew accustomed to not writing her or visiting her as I once regularly did. Until the other day.

I thought of my friend and was once more filled with the sad emptiness I experienced when she died. I thought I had handled all that then, five years ago, I told myself. Which of Elisabeth Kübler-Ross's five stages of grief did I omit or slide through that they should reach out to grab me now, after all this time?

What I gradually realized was that grief—and other feelings as well—aren't events to be experienced or tasks to be completed once and for all. Losses set off a sequence of events. As time passes, we move through our feelings about the initial moment many times, each time from a different perspective or place in time.

—Margot Hover [13]

Novelist Eugenia Price echoes Hover's discovery:

> *Even after six years my heart cries out now and then to my beloved late editor. 'Where are you?' Can't you help me with this chapter? It's tangled—a mess. Do you really know what I'm going through in my work without you?*

> *"Oh, I'm sorry," someone said when Tay died, "but you're established as a writer. You'll find another good editor." I wanted to scream. I did inside. Tay was first of all my friend. My loved one. I love my present fiction editor equally well, but she doesn't try to take Tay's place.*

> —*Eugenia Price* [14]

When the writing gets tough, something within Eugenia calls out for a friend-editor named Tay—just as you too have silently called out to your friend, "If only you were here. . . ."

Reality 1:

Friends will be comforted by opening themselves to thorough grieving. Every hotel I've ever stayed in has little doorknob signs: *"DO NOT DISTURB!"* That's what I need now. A little piece of plastic to hang on my heart while I grieve.

> *You need to give yourself to grief. It does no good to deny it. It does no good to attempt to rationalize it, over-think it, intellectualize it. . . . Grief will have its way.*

> —*Jonathan Lazear* [15]

My advice from experience as a friend-griever as well as a researcher can be summed-up in nine words:

Feel your pain.

Feel *your* pain.

Feel your *pain*.

Make no mistake: Grief will gain your attention. "Nowhere to hide" is accurate. There is no way under it, over it, or around it. One can only go through grief. Sadly, many believe mourning to be pathological or, at least, a weakness to be overcome. We need courageous grievers who will experience their grief without hint of apology and who will. . . . Set the model that mourning is not an illness, is not a weakness, is not a self indulgence or a reprehensible bad habit, but rather, mourning is an essential psychological process which must be recognized and facilitated. Learn to trust your own feelings.

—*Patrick J. Farmer* [16]

But before you can trust them, you've got to feel them! We are designed to grieve our losses. Consider the grief-style of Jesus when his friend Lazarus died:

When they brought Jesus to the place where his dead friend lay, Jesus wept. It is very easy to sentimentalize the scene and very tempting because to sentimentalize it is to look only at the emotion in it and at the emotion it stirs in us rather than at the reality of it, which we are always tempted not to look at because reality, truth, silence are all what we are not much good at and avoid when we can. To sentimentalize something is to savor rather than to suffer the sadness of it . . .

Thus, this author insists, we want to turn Jesus into Gregory Peck or some other strong male figure:

But here standing beside the dead body of his dead friend he is not Gregory Peck. He has no form or comeliness about him that we should desire him, . . . To see a man weep is not a comely sight, especially this man whom we want to be stronger and braver than a man, and the impulse is to turn away from him as we turn from anybody who weeps because the sight of real tears, painful and disfiguring, forces us to look to their source where we not choose to look because where his tears come from, our tears also come.

—*Frederick Buechner* [17]

When I was a child I sang a pleasant little song about Jesus in Sunday school, and about all I remember are the words "He the great example is a pattern for me." We were awarded gold stars—and a hug from Mrs. Greta Quinn—for memorizing scriptures. I received lots of hugs and stars for the verses I memorized. They were in the King James translation, and some of them were rather long! Yet, week after week, my friend David Loser got a gold star for the same verse: "Jesus wept." That was all it took to make Mrs. Quinn weep. Yet over the years David's verse has stuck with me more than the ones I memorized: Jesus—the great teacher—wept. That seemed odd to me at the time, growing up in a family that discouraged crying, at least by males.

Sometimes great theological truths can be captured in simple, anybody-can-understand words. None are more profound, for me, than "Jesus wept," which still sounds too "stained-glassy." I prefer the translation that reads: "Jesus began to cry." Yes, that sounds so human. And I'm sure Jesus offered no "I'm sorry." His grief was as natural as his breath. After all, his friend Lazarus had been dead for four days.

Jesus raised his friend Lazarus from the dead. That act elicited enough animosity from his critics to ensure his own death in the near future. But there is a wonderful addendum to the story. In response to Jesus' word "Lazarus come forth!" Lazarus hobbled out of his tomb, bound in the tightly-wrapped burial cloths. So then Jesus said, "Take off the grave clothes and let him go."

Today, I don't expect my friend to be resurrected, especially since she was cremated. But I need some help getting untangled from my "grave clothes," and from my own emotions and fears and irritation that some have discounted. Hopefully someone will come along soon and unravel me.

I find wise comfort in the following words of grief counselor Doug Manning:

> *Grieving is as natural as crying when you are hurt, sleeping when you are tired, eating when you are hungry, or sneezing when your nose itches. It is nature's way of healing a broken heart.* [18]

Manning goes one step further:

> *Don't let anyone take your grief from you. You deserve it, and*
> *you must have it. If you had broken a leg, no one would criticize*
> *you for using crutches until it was healed. If you had major surgery,*
> *no one would pressure you to run a marathon the next week. Grief*
> *is a major wound. It does not heal overnight. You must have the*
> *time and the crutches until you heal.* [19]

We all probably agree with Manning when it comes to grieving for husbands, wives, parents, and children. But for friends?
Yes for friends! Definitely!

———

> *The level of intimacy between close friends is higher than*
> *many other social relations, including those of biological relatedness.*
> *Friendships which have endured also have greater demands than*
> *from other interests, and so forth. Because of the uniqueness of the*
> *experience of friendship, the death of a friend is a profound loss.*
> *Moving through this grief is often complicated because of the*
> *lack of sensitivity to the need of friends in grief.*
>
> —*Louis F. Kavar* [20]

———

> *But grief still has to be worked through. It is like walking*
> *through water. Sometimes there are little waves lapping about my feet.*
> *Sometimes there is an enormous breaker that knocks me down.*
> *Sometimes there is a sudden and fierce squall.*
>
> —*Madeleine L'Engle* [21]

Why? Because mourning is anchored in relationship. You are
mourning because you invested in a particular friendship that has
been amputated by death. The greater your investment, the more
profound your loss.

The sorrow we feel when we lose someone or something we love is the measure of how valuable he or she or it was to us. The pain is slight if the value was small, great if it was great, immeasurable if it was priceless. A loss would be hardly noticeable, let alone painful, if what was lost was worth nothing.

> *So we would never know suffering if happiness didn't exist.*
> *Sorrow is the price we pay for joy.*
>
> —*Joan Bel Geddes* [22]

Some people choose to live out these left-to-be-lived years in an emotional exile high up on the bank of life—protected, they think, from further loss. So anxious are they to protect their hearts from further and future griefs that they avoid friendships and settle for sterile *acquaintanceships*, of the "Hi. How are you?" variety. They constantly warn themselves: "Don't get too close!" Some people, I have noticed, settle for far less, *nod-ships*—individuals they see occasionally and who only merit a nod and a hinted smile. That's no way to live! Our losses can lead us to a despair-filled, "Who's next?" Three groups particularly ask that question with soul-numbing regularity. They are inner-city adolescents, the elderly, and people who are HIV-positive.

Robert Brown and Rufus Coleman had been friends since junior high. In inner-city Dallas these teens lived with a constant awareness of death through drive-by shootings, robberies, and drug deals gone bad, and the reckless disregard for life. But when Rufus chose to make academics his priority, the friendship changed. Still, when Robert was found dead, Rufus grieved for his friend who did not live long enough to graduate from high school. Rufus expressed his feelings in a powerful essay published in the *Dallas Morning News*:

> *Since then, I've been so lonely. I was so desperate to make some sense of this. Robert and I were no different. I was no different from any of the rest, either. It's like being in the middle of a war and watching your friends go down one by one. But I walked away. And I don't know why. I feel so guilty that I was fortunate enough to survive.*
>
> —*Rufus Coleman* [23]

"Damn death!"
I scream that with exclamation marks
in case death is taking a breather
and can hear me.

I am old.
I can't escape oldness: mine or that of my friends.
I'm not as ready to "kick the bucket" as some assume.
But I am the last of my gang.
Daily life—without my friends—is drudgery.

I read all about George Burns
Still actively doing comedy routines
and getting laughs in his nineties
rather than being laughed at.
Me? "Actively" is too brilliant a word
to describe my existence at Shady Lawn.
"God's waiting room"
that's what they should call the place.
We residents are just waiting for either Ed McMahon
or Mr. Death to come calling.

I've had nine roommates
since I came to Shady Lawn—
started to say moved
but that implies it was my decision.
The occupants of the other bed in this room
confuse my adult children
on their occasional—
very occasional—visits.
"What happened to Mrs. . . ?" they ask.
(They never can remember the names)
"Died." I answer.
"Died?" they repeat.
"Yeah, died. Kicked the bucket. Expired.
Passed on. Passed away . . ."
"You pick the phrase . . ."
Amazing how fast my kids can change the subject.

I've outlived two husbands, two sisters,
one precious little baby, nine roommates and more friends
than I can remember.
And that's why I start every day at Shady Lawn
saying, "Damn death!"
I think death is playing with me cause she knows
I'm one tough ole' gal.
Mess with me and she's got a fight on her hands!
I ain't dying 'til I am good-and-ready and have worn out my welcome
on this planet.
Now, you'll have to excuse me.
I'm waiting for roommate ten to show up.

   —Harold Ivan Smith

Ageism complicates the grieving of many older Americans for their friends who have died. The loss is negated with the cliché, "Well, she lived a good long life." This is sometimes interpreted as, "They were old. What can you expect?" I expect them to hang around to actively participate in my life:

My litany of losses
is far too severe to recite.
Besides, who has time to hear it?
A string of losses make up my grief:
What started with my husband
escalated far too quickly
for my frail heart.
These days funerals and bingo are the major
components of my social life.
Seems like I am always making
a casserole or a pie to take
to the hungerless grieving family.
This slow sifting of longtime friends
like particles of sand
through an hourglass
scours the fragile lining of my soul.
How many more friends can I lose
and still be me?

By the year 1910 Clara Barton, founder of the American Red Cross, was reeling from the deaths of so many of her friends. The *New York World* newspaper asked the humanitarian to identify eight women qualified for the Hall of Fame, prompting her reflection on the deaths. One biographer noted, "Clara was beginning to feel alone in a world of shadows. By winter she was mourning Julia Ward Howe, then her friend Henri Dunant, whom she lamented as "one more of the great and the good gone."

At age ninety Barton wrote:

> *It is remarkable how many persons of prominence, known to the world, are just now passing on. One scarcely thinks on which side to place a friend at first thought. This world begins to seem empty to us who have known and had them so long.*

> —*Clara Barton* [24]

Gay men also share this increased loss; today many feel like they live in a war zone. Many have already lost more friends than their parents have in a lifetime. Ray Russ explained his participation in an AIDS candlelight vigil in San Francisco: "I'm here because I can no longer count on my hands or feet or any other extensions of my body the number of friends I've lost in the past two years." [25] Buss is not talking about casual acquaintances but friends!

Deep in our souls we deplore death's appetite for the young: "It's not supposed to be this way." Ah, *supposed*—a word unknown in death's lexicon. Doris Grumbach, in her eighties, in her memoirs, has disclosed her grief for her many young friends who have died—and her guilt for reaching an age they will never reach. Another mourner noted poignantly of those who have experienced multiple losses:

> *We gay men are living under a pile of corpses that we can't bury emotionally.*

> —*Franklin Abbott* [26]

The gay community must also deal with the stigma imposed on the death of the friends—as indeed must straight friends and family. Rarely have the dead been held-up to such ridicule, paradoxically often by those who claim to follow one described as "a man of sorrows, and familiar with suffering" (Isaiah 53:3). Surely Jesus is still acquainted with grief.

Yet the highest at-risk groups are those friends for whom society has denied acceptable social means for the resolution of grief. Grief must be public to be shared and must be shared to be diminished.

—Jeannette R. Folta and Edith S. Deck [27]

Even when the friend's death is not stigmatized, others rarely comprehend the grief, that is, until it happens to them:

But I do not think that very many people even know how to say, "I'm sorry." One of my best friends got murdered a few months ago. It really hurt me when many of my close relatives and other people acted as if nothing had happened. Maybe they thought that mentioning it to me would hurt me even more. But the worst thing a person can do is never say anything.

—Hannah Sluss [28]

When we grieve for a friend, we are anxious for someone to validate our loss. But three two-letter responses make up the standard repertoire: "Oh," "No," and "So?" The trinity of human response.

What more can people offer the grieving? Who has trained them, empowered them, to walk confidently into a friend's grief? My friend died and all you can say is "Oh"? At least punctuate it with an exclamation mark.

And some hint of a groan. *"OH!"* Sure we've read John Donne's infamous lines, "No man is an island." [29] But we don't do so well with metaphor. Not in a replacement-obsessed culture: "Make some new friends." "So, what's the big deal?"

"Oh, you have lots of friends."
That's what someone said to me
when I told them of Sarah's death.
Although I am blessed by a rich bounty of friends,
I am diminished by the loss of any of them.
No one, these days, has friends to spare.
It would be like saying to a museum curator
after a masterpiece has been stolen
"Oh, you have lots of paintings . . ."
Perhaps.
But I had only one that hung there.

—Harold Ivan Smith

Advice like, "Get a hold of yourself!" may come from surprising sources. Remember, for some, friendships are like carburetors, easily replaced with a minimum of inconvenience. Indeed, some follow this guidance from Lord Byron:

> *Let no man grumble when his friends fall off,*
> *As they will do like leaves at the first breeze:*
> *When your affairs come round, one way or t'other,*
> *Go to the coffee house, and take another.* [30]

"Take another"? I cannot agree with such thinking; in fact, it is disguised denial and certainly counterproductive to healthy healing. I find a healthier perspective in the note penned by Mary Paxton Keeley to her dying friend, Bess Truman, first lady of the United States from 1945 to 1953. The two women had been friends for ninety years! "No one could ever take your place in my life." [31]

Some people would suggest that public mourning is easier for women who have not been socialized in the "take it like a man" school of emotional expression. Consider a chance conversation between two women on a plane:

Flying between two cities, I sit beside a woman who, like me, is reading her manuscript. Neither of us means to speak, and yet we do, sanctioned by coincidence. What are you writing, she asks. Grief, I answer her. She says, My best friend in the world just died. The accident in England: Did you hear? The ferry tipped. I prayed she wasn't on it, but she was.

I still cannot believe that she's not here. I speak then of Lydia, someone I loved for almost twenty years. Of all my friends, I say, Lydia had by far the most vitality. That was my friend's name, Sue tells me quietly. We stare at each other without words.

—*Nessa Rapport* [32]

Could such a conversation have occurred between men?

*Some men do not understand
your grief for a friend because
they have never dared open themselves
to a male friendship.
Instead, they have continually acquiesced
to cultural fears and stereotypes.
Culture's cherished lies block any deep
friendship, let alone grief,
between "real" men.*

*Sadly, most men will wander
through their whole lives
never having known
the intimacy of a true friendship
with another man.
Buddies, yes;
pals
chums
comrades
sidekicks
colleagues
blood kin.
But never friends.*

Too busy
Too afraid
Too desperate
Too unwilling to bend

Too male
Too macho
to be a friend.
Too bad.

They will die impoverished
having defended
the cultural definition
for another generation.
They will die, so short
of their human potential.

—Harold Ivan Smith

Reality 2:

Friends are comforted through tears. Tears punctuate or lubricate our mourning following a friend's death:

> *Tears can be a gentle and loving way of ministering to yourself.*
> *Tears should be honored as tender drops of remembrance.*
>
> *—Lon Nungesser* [33]

You may nod in agreement with a grieving friend who confessed . . .

> *I thought I would run out of tears.*
>
> *—Debra Jarvis* [34]

However, there are still some misshapen notions about men and tears that get in the way of authentic grief. All my life I have been ordered, "Don't cry!" "Dry those tears!" "Take it like a man!" "You don't want people to think you're a sissy." "You're just a cry-baby!" "Only girls cry!" I think that it is about time that I think for myself, especially since I am the one going to all the funerals. Why would it be wrong for me to cry when I have the capacity to cry? Especially, when life has given me so much to cry about? It may not be masculine to cry but it is definitely human.

Not everyone can cry. Doris Grumbach discovered this after the editor of two of her books died. She journaled:

> Oddly, I cannot cry. I am too angry with the God I trusted to save him, to lift his affliction. All the way back to Washington tears press against my eyes, but they never come. Two weeks go by. I do the ordinary household things to ready our home for winter. [35]

Sometimes one's emotions vary from moment to moment, unpredictably. From out of nowhere can come a stimulus that prompts a raid on the memory bank and fresh tears and sadness:

> The next two weeks I cried until there were no more tears. I screamed until my throat was raw. I sulked in silence. I began to relive all the memories of my friends, laughing about the good times, crying about their deaths, allowing my anger because I felt cheated out of saying good-bye to them. I wrote letters to each one, saying the things I wanted to say. I wrote a goodbye to each, and then burned them all. As the smoke rose into the sky, I let my pain rise with it and let it go. The third week I rested, exhausted.
>
> —James P. Bell [36]

Reality 3:

Friends are comforted through routine. Some friends have experienced numbness, especially as they go through established routines. "Just keep busy," we are advised. Some avoid favorite restaurants, shops, or activities. "Too many memories." Anything to keep the grief at bay.

The men sat in silence, and they had ordered their usuals
but most just pushed the food around their plates.
John Kinder was dead.
John Kinder, who had always sat
in the chair nearest the jukebox,
had just up and died on them,
without any warning.
"The picture of health."

Yesterday he ate the breakfast special.
Eggs scrambled, three strips of bacon,
hash browns and biscuits.
Just yesterday morning, for heaven's sake.
As he had every morning he and his buddies gathered here.
This was their table; no one would dare
sit here—well, at breakfast time.
It had been, for years, their sanctuary,
although they could have saved lots of money
as Earl Jr. frequently pointed out—
eating cornflakes in their shorts at home.
This had become their gathering ritual
before starting a workday.
Breakfast, coffee, and "jawing" at the Boar's Head Cafe.

Yesterday John Kinder was here:
eating, teasing, laughing, holding his own;
This morning he's lying in the front parlor at Gilbert and Sons,
five blocks down Main Street.
They'd all been down there last night although they'd spent more time
talking on the porch than standing in the parlor.
Yes they'd gone to pay their respects
but more to verbalize their disbelief
that death could just barge in
and claim their friend.
No one wanted to come this morning;
No one dared stay away.

So they sat mostly in silence
sneaking glances
at John Kinder's empty chair,
mourning.

—Harold Ivan Smith

In writing this book, I have reexamined my attitudes on the stoic male and concluded the following:

Just because I'm not saying anything
doesn't mean that I'm not grieving.
Words just cannot capture my loss—
at least not any words I know.
Why he was my best friend!
I'd been knowing him for nearly forty-five years.
How is a man supposed to put that into words?
And how is a man supposed to imagine a world
without such a friend?

Reality 4:

Friends are comforted by anger, as one friend wrote:

Of course I am upset! I have lost a friend such as will never be seen again. Or so I must assume. For of this at least I am sure: there has never been a friend like him before. [37]

Poet Maya Angelou suggests that anger is not always an initial reaction but shows up on it's own schedule.

I can accept the idea of my own demise, but I am unable to accept the death of anyone else. I find it impossible to let a friend or relative go into that country of no return. Disbelief becomes my close companion, and anger follows in its wake.

—Maya Angelou [38]

"This doesn't make any sense!" A friend's death can be one of the most illogical acts—and that reality may greatly complicate the grieving. Arlene Shannon faced this when her friend Ron Phillips, a United Methodist minister, was killed by a parishioner in 1993 in front of a stunned congregation.

Arlene had worked with Ron in the large single adult ministry in St. Luke's United Methodist Church in Indianapolis, where Ron was well-loved by the single adults. Early in her grieving, Arlene eulogized her friend, "Ron Phillips, you get an A+ for your considerable efforts on behalf of St. Luke's Singles." Arlene did more. She attended the murder trial, "hoping to salvage something that would allow others to grow from this tragedy." Arlene also made herself available to the angry single adults friends who called or stopped by her office for updates. The question remained for many of Ron's friends, "How could God let this happen to Ron, a minister?" [39] Arlene learned, as have many, that a friend's murder is a hard emotional wound to heal. Indeed, every stage—arrest (if there is an arrest), conviction (if there is a conviction), the appeals, and parole hearings—keep re-injuring the griever.

The grief-wound gets re-injured by those who try to negate or interrupt our grief with perhaps, well-intentioned admonitions: "He's with the Lord." Or "He's in a better place." "We just don't understand the ways of the Lord." Archbishop Desmond Tutu faced the last statement when his friend, activist Steve Biko, was killed while in the detention of South African police. Tutu, however, had to confront his questions in his sermon to 15,000 people gathered in a soccer stadium for Biko's funeral:

> *When we heard the news "Steve Biko is dead" we were struck numb with disbelief. No, it can't be true! No, it must be a horrible nightmare and we will awake and find in reality that it is different— that Steve is alive even if it be in detention. But no, dear friends, he is dead and we are struck with anguish. Oh God, where are you? Oh, God, do you really care? How can you let this happen to us?*

I suspect Tutu's three questions for God are universally spoken or felt by friends. Tutu added the following:

It all seems such a waste of a wonderfully gifted person, struck down in the bloom of youth, a youthful bloom that some wanted to see blighted. What can be the purpose of such wanton destruction? God, do you really love us?

—*Desmond Tutu* [40]

Tutu's question is a question asked by almost all grievers: "God, do you really care for me in my loss?" It can be difficult, as Tutu discovered, to be a spokesperson for the Almighty. One Catholic priest explained:

I miss them. Their deaths are a painful loss. Whenever I think of them, I feel a biting pain that they are no longer in their homes with their families and friends. I can no longer call them, visit them, hear their voices or see their faces. I feel immense grief. But I believe deeply that their deaths are more than a loss. Their deaths are also a gift.

—*Henri Nouwen* [41]

How does a friend handle anger?

When I sense myself filling with rage at the absence of my beloved, I try as soon as possible to remember that my concerns and questions, my effort and answers should be focused on what I did or can learn from my departed. . . . What legacy was left which can help me in the art of living a good life?

If I employ the legacies of my late beloveds, I am certain death will take itself and me as well.

—*Maya Angelou* [42]

Reality 5:

Friends are comforted by the struggle with the "Why?" question and the struggle to let go. That principle sounds oxy-moronic. Some people will challenge this by saying, "Hardly. I am uncomforted by the struggle."

I can't find any relief. Too many things remind me of my friend and of our friendship. I am doing well and then, without warning, I fall through some trapdoor. C. S. Lewis, not usually known as a slobbering sentimentalist, observed the following:

> *Walking To-day by a cottage I shed tears*
> *When I remembered how once I had walked there*
> *With my friends who are mortal and dead.*
> *Little had healed the wound that was laid bare.*
>
> *Out little spear that stabs! I, fool, believed*
> *I had outgrown the local, unique sting,*
> *I had transmuted wholly (I was deceived)*
> *Into Love universal the lov'd thing.* [43]

Emotions have a way of wrecking havoc on our lives; we try to go about this in an civil manner but are blindsided, emotionally ambushed. Our grief demands, "Now! What about me?!" Often grief is complicated by absence of permission to grieve. Friends need someone to say, "Go right ahead and grieve." Until friendgrief is fully recognized by morticians, ministers, florists, personnel directors, and greeting card manufacturers, we may well continue to grieve in what could be labeled, an "emotional wilderness."

Too often we can't let go because to let go now would be premature; we will be unable to fully let go until we have done the reflective grieving and asked our "Why?"s.

> *Inevitably our anguish fills the question, "Why?" if not on our lips, then in our hearts. There is no answer that removes this question—no answer that can bridge the chasm of irreparable separation. Life will never be the same, and this is at it should be, for our loved ones are not expendable.*
>
> *—Paul Carnes* [44]

Repeatedly asking "Why?" is an essential element in the healing, although not everyone is willing to wait for the reflective answers to unravel. We want answers now!

Three good people died in the middle of their lives and through no
fault of their own, and I find myself asking why they died, and
discovering that the answers that used to comfort me are suddenly out
of date. . . . In the year that has passed since the first of these deaths, my
philosophies have regained none of their power to comfort and explain.

The terrible truths have lost none of their power either—though the
shock is gone—and my world will never be quite the same.

—*Phillip Yancey* [45]

The reflection on the question "Why?" can impact every dimen-
sion of the personhood of an individual struggling with friendgrief.
No wonder people run from grief.

Every meal with my family, every walk with my wife, every
chance to untangle a paragraph or talk to a child or search for galax-
ies on a clear night—all have a sharper edge than before, a subtle
urgency, an air of passing away that makes me want to take all the
chances that come along, and keep my eyes and ears wide open and
my mouth more often closed, so that I miss nothing. I have less time
to waste on anger, or on the endless enterprises of being vindicated
and being understood.

—*Michael Nesset* [46]

Fortunately poets and philosophers have not hesitated to
engage the distressing "Why?"

I am besieged with painful awe at the vacuum left by the dead.
Where did he go? Where is she now? Are they, as the poet James Weldon
Johnson said, "resting in the bosom of Jesus?" If so, what about my
Jewish loves, my Japanese dears, and my Muslim darlings? Into whose
bosom are they cuddled? There is always, lurking quietly, the question
of what certainty is there that I, even I, will be gathered into the gentle
arms of the Lord. I start to suspect that only with such blessed assur-
ance will I be able to allow death its duties.

—*Maya Angelou* [47]

Maybe grieving is easier for those who relish the sentimental approach, or who go emotionally berserk for a few days or weeks and get it out of their systems.

> *You won't like the way your loss makes you feel. Although we can't control our emotions, we can control our response to them. Know that no matter how guilty you may feel over how the intensity of your feelings seems to make other people feel, you own those feelings; they are yours to experience and express freely.*
>
> *In other words, it's OK to grieve.*
>
> *—Lon Nungesser* [48]

Country music singer Reba McIntire was criticized by many fans in 1991, when only nine days after her entire band had been killed in a plane crash she sang at the Academy Awards. That appearance was part of her struggle—her friends would have wanted it that way. After all, "the show must go on." One difficulty of friends' deaths is trying to find in our previous experiences with grief something to help us initially cope with and eventually survive this loss. Two years after the accident, Reba told an interviewer:

> *[My] divorce was tough, but it was nothing compared with the crash. It was the worse time in my life. It still causes a knot in my throat to talk about it.*
>
> *—Reba McIntire* [49]

Maybe that's why we don't talk about our friendgrief. Why we abruptly change the subject and rely on a pronoun, *he* or *she*, to avoid saying the deceased's name. The words would have to pole vault over the knot in our throats and hearts. Abigail Adams, the second First Lady of the United States, used another metaphor to capture her loss after the death of her friend Will Smith in April 1816: "Although it can be but a short time before I shall follow him, I feel a limb lop'd from the body." [50]

A fresh outbreak of grief can be triggered by something as simple as spotting a name in an address book or the space where a name used to be, or finding the last card from a friend in a stack of old holiday or birthday cards we meant to discard long ago.

My friend Martin was not afraid of dying. My friend was afraid that he would too soon be forgotten. After all, isn't that the way we are busily occupied in the business of replacing? So, in those last days, over and over again, I reassured him that as long as I had my wits about me and I had my memories, I would replay them over and over, perhaps in slow motion, and through the tears find the courage to laugh. And after the laughing I would find gratitude for having been privileged to have had such a friend.

Part of the struggle is linguistic: getting the verbs in correct tense. Is it "I had" or "I have" a friend? Isn't even the structure of that last question wrong? Had . . . ? No, I still have him as a friend.

In our last conversations he nettled me: "Oh, you'll make some new friends . . ."

"No!" I snapped, leaving him speechless. "I don't simply scratch out names in either my address book or my heart and insert new ones, as if there are only so many slots available on my friend-ship roster." My battered address book, held together now with a large rubber band, merited replacing long ago, but I cannot find it in my heart to dispense with it.

There are still names for whom addresses and phone numbers are long irrelevant but which remain there, as in my memory, because I do not want to white them out just yet; my grief is too raw. Unfortunately, some friends sabotage their grief work by making it too cerebral:

> *Some survivors try to think their way through grief. That doesn't work. Grief is a releasing process, a discovery process, a healing process. We cannot release or discover or heal by the use of our minds alone. The brain must follow the heart at a respectful distance. It is our hearts that ache when a [friend] loved one dies. Certainly, the mind suffers, the mind recalls, the mind may plot and wish, but it is the heart that will blaze the trail through the thicket of grief.*

> —*Carol Staudacher* [51]

Loss is mastered not by forgetting the past or holding on to it but by abstracting from it the essential meaning of the tie and recreating it to fit a whole new life which must go on without the missing [friend].

—Bertha Simos [52]

The reflective process and the hard work that loss demands convinces many people that mourning is more of a spiral than a five-step process.

Whatever grief means to us, or however we understand the grief process, it may be reassuring to view it in terms of a spiral, where we encounter or view those feelings many times, each time from a different vantage point. That's different from the linear view, where one climbs out of one's feelings, and where their return is viewed as a kind of back-sliding. Emotions don't get "finished"; they visit us many times, each time at a different level.

—Margot Hover [53]

Reality 6:

Friends are comforted through the gentle kindnesses of caring people in ordinary and extraordinary moments. Some of us, even when bogged down in the thicket of grief, cannot ask for help. Like impatient two-year-olds we insist, "I can do it myself!" While you must grieve your way and at your speed, you will not grieve healthily without support. And you may be surprised by the sources of help available.

You want to know who has helped me?
That's easy.
It wasn't the folks with the answers
or the folks with the pious clichés
and platitudes or
the folks with the advice.
No. It was those precious people
who listened all the way

to the end of my sentences
even when those babbled sentences
did not have periods.
It was those precious people
who let me sob and slobber
and moan and wail
and who simply sat with me
staring into the bottom of a coffee cup
as if the answers I needed
might be hiding there.
It was those who listened and nodded
and patted and hugged
and wept and waited with me
for this season called grief
to end.

—Harold Ivan Smith

I encountered an unexpected grace
today at Raceland Mall, of all places!
I ran into Carolyn
and she was not deterred
by my polite attempts at chit-chat
in order to avoid "It."
"Let's find a place to talk" she insisted,
vetoing my initial reserve.
So, across from Chic-Filet and Cinema 6
we made a temporary oasis
out of the traffic flow
of shoppers doing their mall-ing.

"I've been thinking about you."
"Me?"
"Yes. I know that Betty's death has been . . ."
she paused, reassembling her thoughts,
"Ah, hard, harder on you . . ."
All I could get out was, "She was my best
friend and I miss her so . . ."

The dam broke; the words and tears surged
out in a verbal raging flow.
In the middle of the mall I lost the control
I had worked so hard to maintain.
I realized I was in a safe place.

After I composed myself, somewhat,
I looked around and gestured:
"Here is where I miss her the most."
Carolyn did not need an explanation but I
launched into one.
We spent hours here . . . not always buying,
just being together, eating, laughing,
knowing how our husbands would tease us,
"And who was the reigning Queen of the Mall today?"
We took turns reigning.

I always trusted her judgment.
My husband said it was easier on his money
when I shopped alone.
I always checked the price tag, first.
More than once she'd slap my hand, "Stop that!"
How many times did Betty say—in one breath—
"Honey, it's you" and to the clerk, "We'll take it."
More than once Carolyn talked me into clothes
that earned incredible compliments.

"Now," I said softly, "I shop alone—
when I even shop.
All the fun's gone out of it.
Anywhere in this mall, I can see her."

We would have talked longer
but the movie had ended
and patrons were loudly streaming out
and some folks in the Chic Filet line
were aggressively eyeing our bench.

But, I felt better because Carolyn listened
all the way to the end of my sentences.
Perhaps our bumping into each other
was merely a coincidence.
I think not.
Whatever, Carolyn volunteered to be my mall "buddy"
"Anytime" she insisted.
I may just take her up on that.

—Harold Ivan Smith

Grief has a way of sneaking up on you. It comes in the middle of a very ordinary experience or in the middle of an extraordinary moment when you so wish your friend could share the experience, either in person or later in conversation. "If only he could see me now!" Nelson Mandela struggled with such thoughts on May 10, 1994, as he was inaugurated president of South Africa:

I was overwhelmed with a sense of history. That day had come about through the unimaginable sacrifices of thousands of my people, people whose suffering and courage can never be counted or repaid. I felt that day, as I have on many other days, that I was simply the sum of all those African patriots who had gone before me. . . . I was pained that I was not able to thank them and that they were not able to see what their sacrifices had wrought. . . .

The decades of oppression and brutality . . . produced the Oliver Tambos, the Walter Sisulus, the Chief Luthulis, the Yosaf Davaos, the Bram Fishers, the Robert Sobukwes of our time—men of such extraordinary courage, wisdom, and generosity that their likes may never be known again. It is from these comrades that I learned the meaning of courage. [54]

While writing this book, I took a month off and went to France and Italy with my friend Greg. Our mutual friend, John Culver, had died ten months before, disappointed that his illness had forced him to jettison his adult long-planned trip to Paris. How many times did Greg say—his voice heavy with regret—"John would have loved this . . ." John's sister Nancy had sent us money from his estate to enjoy a fine meal in Paris in memory of John. So one spring evening in a wonderful little restaurant in the Sixth Arrondissement, we toasted the life and memory of John. Grievers need such moments.

I have not always appreciated lighting candles in sacred places until one rainy Saturday on that trip. In the great cathedral at Chartres, I was drawn to the candles, as had many that day (confirmation had drawn a full house). The glow from the tall white burning tapers was mystical. As I lifted my candle to light it from the flame of another griever's candle, their names paraded through my soul: Rusty, Martin, Bud, John M., Anne, Cecil, Leon, Lois, Bunny, John. . . . It was a tenderly holy moment. In trips past, I had "remembered" them with "Having a great time . . . wish you were here" postcards. But in the silence of that moment I was reminded that the sentiments were the same: "Having a great time . . . oh, how I wish you were still here."

Recently, John's sister gave birth to a boy. I had a present to send but wanted to write a few lines to a little guy who will grow up without his uncle, my friend. One morning I sat down at my lap-top computer intending to "dash out" a note, but thoughts kept jumping up and down in my brain demanding to be included:

Elliott Culver Keller:

> *Welcome to planet Earth. Glad you arrived safe and sound. Well, that's quite a name your parents gave you but it's a strong sounding name. Elliott, I am sorry that you won't get to know your uncle John— at least for a while. You would have loved him and oh, how he would have loved you. He was a kind, caring, gentle man. He had a wonderful big heart and he loved music and Karen Carpenter and Ethyl Merman and people. And your uncle John made this world a better place. And a lot of people miss your uncle John a whole lot. I wouldn't be writing you this letter if I had not known your uncle John.*

The following is what I did not include in the letter, but will eventually tell Elliott:

I am a far better person for John Culver's all-too-brief
appearance as a friend in my life.

Is there a particular point when the mourning is done? Finished? Over? Some would answer a determined yes; others report the reconciliation with the loss as an afterthought—something they just one day recognized was behind them. But for many, particularly those who had experienced rich friendships across a span of years, the grieving is never completed. The friend-shaped hole in the heart never quite heals.

When someone we love dies, a part of us is gone.
We will never, ever, be the same.

—*Ted Menten* [55]

I need to let you know
that you were not replaceable.
You were a one-of-a-kind,
a one-in-a-lifetime friend.
The friendship we had cannot be duplicated.
Indeed, those who audition for my friendship
will have to measure up
to the standard you set.
A high standard.
But my hunch is that eventually
someone will happen by
who has some quality
that will remind me
of your irreplacableness
so a new friendship will be formed.
Not a replacement but a new friendship.

—*Harold Ivan Smith*

People are like puzzles,
and when someone special dies,
there's a feeling that those particular pieces
will never be assembled again—
that particular picture is gone.

—Jonathan Lazear [56]

"She was *just* a friend." That's what you will hear. What will go unsaid is far more crude: "What's the big deal?" "Why are you carrying on so?" Here's one answer to consider: "If I have to explain it to you, you won't understand." Most likely, those who question your grief have never lost such a friend.

When I review those friends whose absence is so conspicuous in my life—especially when good things happen and I want to share the news—I am convinced that should I make humankind's mean of threescore plus ten, I will go to my grave missing my friends. Some unknown griever was accurate when she or he wrote, "When we lose a friend we die a little." [57]

I write my obituaries carefully and think about
how little the facts suffice, not only to describe the dead but to tell
what they will mean to the living all the rest of our lives.
We are defined by who we have lost.

—Anna Quindlen [58]

When Vilma Bansky, a silent film star of the 1920s, died in Los Angeles on March 18, 1991, after a ten-year illness, she left a strange request. Since none of her friends had visited during her illness, the actress ordered that there be no public announcement of her death. Only eighteen months later was Miss Banksky's death finally disclosed. [59]

Closure. Being finished. Some of us approach grief the way we approached final exams—we only knew we were through answering because we had run out of room on the page. A "whew!" came across our lips; we were done. One morning over my eggs and biscuits, I was stunned by Anna Quindlen's words on the opinion page of the *Kansas City Star*:

> *The world loves closure, loves a thing that can, as they say, be gotten through. This is why it comes as a great surprise to find that loss is forever, that two decades after the event there are those occasions when something in you cries out at the continual presence of an absence.*

> —*Anna Quindlen* [60]

Ah, I thought, this writer understands mourning. Her last line, "the continual presence of an absence," proved that she had walked the trail. I folded my paper, paid my bill, and walked out into the spring morning, glad that I was not alone. In an unexpected place, I had been reminded that I was not alone in choosing to honor my dead friends.

The apostle Paul asked, "Death, where is thy sting?"—a question that has been starting point for many a funeral sermon. I like Maya Angelou's response: "It is here in my heart and mind and memories." [61]

When Saigon fell on April 30, 1975, this nation breathed a collective sigh of relief. The Vietnam War was over, at last. Or so we thought. Two decades later, the arguments over Bill Clinton's (and other presidential aspirants') draft status and the disputed decision to normalize relations with Vietnam were subtle reminders that the mourning for the thousands of Americans who had died there was not over. When the book *In Retrospect*—the repentant Vietnam memoirs of former defense secretary Robert McNamara—was published in April 1975, the effect was like a match on gasoline-soaked wood. Vietnam was again center stage on the American consciousness. From radio talk shows, to the letters to the editor, to the five-thirty national news, people were again giving their grief its voice. The scab had effectively been peeled off the nation's wound. A media frenzy resulted. Next to my laptop, is one of those gruesome

Vietnam photos: four G.I.'s tugging a wounded, perhaps dying, comrade to an evacuation helicopter. Full-page, in color. *Time* magazine noted, "Suddenly, hot arguments over the justice of that war resumed as if interrupted only by a pause for breath, rather than the passage of decades." [62]

So it is with grief. Just biding it's time.

———

Tobias Wolff's stint in Vietnam led to his book *In Pharaoh's Army*. *Time* magazine asked Wolff to respond to McNamara's disclosure. Wolff focused on his experience in a men's group based on Vietnam. "We came together with the best will in the world, but as soon as we began to talk, it grew obvious that our experiences had opened distances between us that no amount of goodwill could bridge." [63] Wolff found that the men who had stayed home could not, in a support-group setting, follow the others to "the outpost of remembrance." "Our histories slammed down between us" and sabotaged communication, let alone healing.

Wolff concluded the essay conceding that things are different now in Ho Chi Minh City: capitalism has found its beachhead. Indeed, vets are going back to launch business ventures; others are vacationing there. On a recent trip to Vietnam, one of Wolff's friends said:

> *Visited the scene of the worse memories in the company of a former NVA officer who'd led an attack against his unit. There they were, together, walking the ground where they had tried to kill each other and where friends of theirs had died. And at the end of the day they managed to do what we at home have yet learned to do. They shook hands.* [64]

Mourning is about the hard work of befriending your grief:

> *Pain pushes you, sometimes gently, sometimes forcefully,*
> *but always in the direction of healing and growth.*

> —*Amy Dean* [65]

"Blessed are those who mourn" thoroughly.

> *Almighty God,*
> *Father of mercies and giver of comfort:*
> *Deal graciously, we pray, with all who mourn;*
> *that, casting all their care on you,*
> *they may know the consolation of your love;*
> *Amen.*
>
> *—-adapted from Book of Common Prayer* [66]

> *We do not ask you*
> *to give us forgetfulness*
> *or to replace [name] with a new friend.*
> *Rather, we ask you*
> *to witness this loss, these fear-filled tears.*
> *To observe our woundedness*
> *and, in time, to applaud our mourning.*
> *Grant us the measure of graced courage*
> *we need to authentically grieve*
> *in a culture that will pressure us*
> *to "move on" or to "get over it."*
>
> *For the gift of friendship*
> *and for a particular friend*
> *named _____.*
> *We give you thanks. Amen.*
>
> *—Harold Ivan Smith*

THE REMEMBERING

I am richer
for having known you.
The world called memory
is brighter
by your presence.
Oh some will say
you are gone
but I know—
know
that you, my friend,
are as close as ever.

Your pain still hangs in air;
Sharp notes of if suspended;
The voice of your despair—
That also is not ended.

When near your death a friend
Asked you what he could do,
"Remember me," you said.
We will remember you.

—*Thomas Gunn* [1]

But how do we keep that promise? If we remember, it hurts. How do we remember in a culture that has made the denial of death into an art form?

Human beings are alone in imagining their deaths; they are also unique in their need to remember the dead and to keep on imaging them. Central to this act of memory is the name of the deceased, that familiar formula of identity by which a person seems to live on after life is over. To forget a name is in effect to allow death to have the last word.

—*Peter S. Hawkins* [2]

I marvel at the capacity of memory.
Which, in some deep pocket
Of my mind, preserves you whole—
As wind is wind, as the lion-taming
Sun is sun, you are, you stay:
Nothing is lost, nothing has blown away.

—*Barbara Howes* [3]

If we are loved and remembered,
then we live on forever in the hearts of those who love us.

—*Ted Menten* [4]

Even the death of friends will inspire us as much as their lives.
. . . Their memories will be entrusted over the sublime and
pleasing thoughts, as monuments of other men are overgrown
with moss; for our friends have no place in the graveyard.

—*Henry David Thoreau* [5]

To lose a friend is the greatest of all evils, but endeavor rather
to rejoice that you possessed him than to mourn his loss.

—*Seneca* [6]

I am not interested in "embalming" the memory of my friends; one embalming was quite sufficient. Rather, I want the vibrant memories of the friendships to be the raw materials for future growth and for new friendships—not to replace friends gone but instead to complement those friendships, which are only "on hold" at the moment. Quite candidly, I am still working on the verbs. I have not gotten used to saying "I had a friend named Rusty" because I believe I still have a friend named Rusty and that I will see him again.

Knowing the living God means knowing why it it is reasonable to hope
that one will survive the grave. Concomitantly, it is finding a reason
to hope that all the precious relationships we developed on earth
will be preserved in heaven.

—John Carmody [7]

Some things cannot easily be explained.
They belong to a realm called faith.
How can I speak of an unending or
never-ending friendship
when I've just come from my friend's
fresh grave?
Although all my intellect tells me that
such thinking, such a hope is fantasy,
of a variety best jettisoned in childhood.
Well, I have chosen to believe
that my friendship still exists,
that my friendship waits to be resumed.
I have chosen to believe my friends are with me
not merely in a memory slice
but in a realm
for which the English language
has not yet created adequate vocabulary.

—Harold Ivan Smith

Some of us are reluctant to be too verbal about our belief in eternal life; hence, we can be surprised by hearing or reading another's perspective:

> *It would help, oh, how it would help if we could have an actual address, a telephone number, but we have the word of God that this recent, hard good-bye is temporary. Nothing hard that happens on earth is for ever.*
>
> —*Eugenia Price* [8]

In my doctoral research, I worked with fifteen individuals who had had a friend die. I asked them, "Do you hope to see your friend again?" One participant, Jeff Black, eloquently expressed his conviction with an "Oh yes!" I asked why he believed that enough to punctuate the conclusion with an exclamation mark. I memorized his answer to enhance my own beliefs: "I can't imagine God going to all that trouble to make such a wonderful friend as Jim and knit together such a wonderful relationship and then just drop it!" [9] A deep need exists to remember the friend.

No love, no friendship can cross the path of our destiny
without leaving some mark on it forever.

—*François Mauriac* [10]

> *People don't leave life until you stop thinking about them.*
>
> —*Larry McMurtry* [11]

Friendship can often impact belief. For example, writer Philip Yancey's belief in Easter and resurrection is shaped by the death of three close friends in separate accidents within a one-year period:

> *One reason I am open to belief, I admit, is that at a very deep level I want the Easter story to be true. Faith grows out of the subsoil of yearning, and something instinctive in human beings cries out against the reign of Death. Whether hope takes the form of Egyptian*

pharaohs stashing their jewels and chariots in pyramids, or the modern American obsession with keeping bodies alive until the last possible nanosecond and then preserving them with embalming fluids in double-sealed caskets, we humans resist the idea of death having the final say. We want to believe otherwise.

I remember the year I lost three close friends in separate accidents. Above all else, I want Easter to be true because of its promise that some-day I will get my friends back.

I believe in the resurrection primarily because I have gotten to know God. I know that God is love, and I also know that we human beings want to keep alive those whom we love. I do not let my friends die; they live on in my memory and my heart long after I have stopped seeing them. . . . God will not let death win.

—*Philip Yancey* [12]

Medical researcher Ronald Valdiserri has been touched by not only the death of his twin brother but also by friends and colleagues. His words compliment Yancey:

I feel a fervent longing to be reunited with those I have loved, those who have left my life after many years of loving or too few. I have come to think of the afterlife as an opportunity to love better and longer than I have been able to do on this earth. Whether I have wings or can hear celestial choirs of harmonizing angels doesn't matter to me. Being able to love and to be loved into eternity is the most won-drous thing I can imagine. [13]

Bill Nichols has been deliberate in remembering his friends, in facilitating that continued presence in his life:

There is something else which has sustained me. In our bedroom is a bookshelf wall. One long shelf there contains only small, framed photographs. Some are of Mariethe [Bill's late wife] of course, some of us together. But dominating the shelf are many pictures of our dearest friends. Pictures through the years, very informal, taken in all sorts of places and with an infinite variety of costumes and postures. It faces our bed—and so it is the first thing I see in the morning, the last thing at night.

Most of the friends in the snapshots are gone now—to Mariethe's Other Side. Soon the rest of us will be going, too. But it really isn't necessary to take time out to debate the exact nature of that Other Side. Let the theologian worry about the specifics of heaven and hell and the sex of angels.

All we need to know is that the people we love—those deep in our memories and our hearts—are waiting for us there. Yet, at the same time, they are also with us here. This is the miracle. The miracle of love.

—William Nichols [14]

I applaud Nichols's example. Each of us must create ways to keep the memories of friends fresh. From reading, I have discovered a wide variety of avenues for active, deliberate remembering. One important way to remember is visiting the grave, which certainly for some friends is a bittersweet experience.

Want to know a little secret?
I eat with dead people. Quite often.
I've had my fill of eating alone
in the fast food joints;
Seeing people, watching me
like I was a troublesome reminder
of some unpleasant fear.
"Hey, pops. How you doin'?"
"Pops." I hate that word!

So I often make a sandwich
and drive out to Parklawn—
after all, I am a property owner there.
It's an old cemetery, generally deserted.
I find a bench, sit, and eat my sandwich.

A few brazen squirrels come close enough
to catch a tossed morsel and keep me company.
Pretty place. Beautiful trees and flowers,
especially in the fall.
And oh, the tranquillity.
It's the right place to practice remembering.
I've seen those slow possessions
creep through the gated entrance to Parklawn,
twist and turn and finally stop
near an open gash in the grass.
I've watched the black-clad folks stand
some under, most near the sheltering green tent.
Often, I compose little stories
about the mourners, especially those
relegated to the perimeter. Wonder why?
I've recognized myself a time or two,
in the persons standing
at the edge of the tent, the friends;
the best seats, of course,
are reserved for the family.
I know. Loneliest ride in my life
was when I brought John Ed here.
Only time in my life I ever rode in a limousine.

Lots of folk would be horrified
to know this is where I spend my time.
They would rather I'd be playing bridge or
riding around on a church van on yet another outing—
the realities of growing old.

They would rather I be walking in circles
through some mall than here.
But I'd rather be here with my friends.
Some days, as I walk around,
I call out names and even wave.
It helps me punctuate this reality called grief.
It's good exercise for my soul and my feet.

—Harold Ivan Smith

Catholic priest Henri Nouwen recommends regular cemetery visits and suggests picnicking there.

> *How often do we go to the cemetery and stand, kneel, or sit in front of the place where our . . . friends have been buried? Are we still in touch with those who have died, or are we living our lives as if those who lived before us never really existed?* [15]

Writer Joyce Rupp noted the following:

> *I was out in the country on an autumn evening going to visit friends on a farm. It was soon after the death of a friend of mine and the pain of loss was still extremely intense. As I walked up the sidewalk in the dusk, I heard the sound of geese flying south. I paused to be still and to listen. The sound of their Southern flight filled me with tears of recognition. At the same time the strong image of geese in transition brought a twinge of hope in my heart. "How much a part of life," I thought, "is this going-away thing. My friend's home is with you, God. I cannot keep wanting to have her here with me in the way she used to be." I walked to the door that night with my first real acceptance of my friend's death. The ache returned many times, but each time it did, I could recall the evening that I paused to pray goodbye as I heard the geese winging their way south.* [16]

Some remembering places are symbolic, like the Vietnam Veterans Memorial in Washington, D.C. Although no one is buried there, "The Wall" has become a sanctuary of friendship for those who served and for those who did not serve.

When I'm in Washington, I often jog to The Wall—early, before the tourists are out. I go to the "Book of Names," look up Donnie's name on the panel-identifier and then walk to the panel and slowly run my finger down the list on 20E until I find his name: Donnie Mesarosh, my friend. And somehow, whatever my business in Washington, I find my mind returning to that summer of '67 when Donnie earned in niche in The Wall.

This war-opposed college student precariously clinging to my deferment only because boys like Donnie had gone to the hellhole of a no-win politician's war, while I wrote papers, took tests, planned a future worrying about little other than my dating life and draft status. I came home one weekend from summer school and was hardly in the back door when my mother announced: "That Mesarosh boy is dead. He's at Heady's." She gestured to the folded obituary section of the *Courier-Journal* on the kitchen table.

How many times did I reread the obit hoping that another reading would somehow make it plainer to me how a good friend could die in a rice paddy while I studied? My agenda for that weekend was swiftly rearranged; I found myself uncomfortably standing in a parlor at Heady's. Most of the time I stood with my back to the casket so I would not be as reminded of its reality.

Early mornings in Washington, after my paused remembrance at The Wall, I go about my business a little more in touch with eternal reality. Why do I come back to the monument? Something soulful beckons me. Something like a hunger for atonement draws me there. Something mystical deep within my being erupts to demand that I take, *make* the time to remember my friend, Donnie.

For some friends, The Wall is overwhelming:

> *This is the final resting place for the spirits of my buddies, their names carved into rock. I'd like to say that I don't care where their bodies lie, but can't. This wall, this black granite, inscribed with end-less names, is all that I have left of my Vietnam brothers—the ones who left their lives "over there."*

> *I stare into the names through the blackness and see their faces—blank in death. Yet they are alive in spirit and as fresh in life as the day they left.*

> *My buddies are right before me screaming the silent closed-mouth scream of death. I stand before them and they stand before me, this black sheet of granite the great dividing wall between the coming-home-me and the coming-home-them.*

> *We touch hands through the wall as touching through a glass window. I feel this tremendous energy pulling me back into them and they to me.*

We silently remain buddies, respectful of the distances between us that can't be broken. They are prisoners within the earth, behind this Wall of black granite. Silently we commune.

I want to scream at everyone around me to get the hell out. "Leave, leave me alone in this graveyard—this is sacred ground." "Stop gawking, go away all you tourists."

I want to be alone with my buddies. I want to talk to them, in silence.

As I kneel before the wall with tears slowly trickling down my cheeks, one woman wants to know if I had friends in Vietnam. I can't believe her rudeness. I wouldn't walk up to her as she kneeled before a headstone in a cemetery and ask her if she knew the person. [17]

A particular place can become a sanctuary we have designated as a place for remembering:

Perhaps I am truly at home when I am at peace with myself, surrounded by the serenity that comes from the Cove, a quiet so deep I am able to hear the roar of the sea in my inner ear, to see in my mind's eye absent friends as well as the dead I have loved, to taste on the buds of fantasy the great meals I am no longer able to digest, to restore the scraps of a quiescent past long buried in my memory by an overactive present.

—*Doris Grumbach* [18]

Some choose to avoid the places so memory-linked with friendship. Yet, there can be those moments when we feel drawn back, en route, praying that we will have the strength to face the reality:

I am flooded with memories.
Here. This particular place.
This particular memory-drenched
strand of beach.
The silent stream of sand through my fingers
stimulates the memories
assembling in the staging area.

He sat there. I sat here.
Two readers catching a few rays.
Finally, he asked, "Is that any good?"
referring to the bestseller I was reading.
So, the afternoon conversation flowed
beyond this new bestseller through
literature as easily, as perhaps for others,
sports, politics, or investments.

Now he's gone. Dead.
Clearly he's not away. Dead.
So this beach, this winter day,
offers only memories—
memories of talking about the books
we each wanted to write,
books that are now up to me to write.
Still I pause for a moment of gratitude:
That on this beach so many years ago
a friendship began that is, at the moment, merely in limbo.

Thankfully, I am certain that our conversation
will be resumed in eternity's day with the simple words,
"Now, where were we?"
About this, I have no doubt.

—*Harold Ivan Smith*

I was stunned, a year after writing the above, to discover that Helen Keller had come to the same conclusion:

> . . . *could not have borne the loss of such an intimate and tender friend if I had thought he was indeed dead. But his noble philosophy and certainty of the life to come braced me with an unwavering faith that we should meet again in a world happier and more beautiful than anything of my dreaming.* [19]

This is, quite frankly, a lot to believe: friendships and conversations, begun here, resumed in eternity with little notice of a pause? Surely you don't really believe that? Well, it's one of those ideas that I have chosen not to be too vocal about. I want neither to be challenged nor dismissed. I simply need this belief. But my cowardice in revealing what really is a dogged-determined belief may keep others from believing. Imagine my relief when I stumbled across this quotation posed by Frederick Buechner:

> *I have always loved fairy tales and to this day I read E. Nesbitt and the Oz books, Andrew Lang and the Narnia books and Tolken with more intensity than I read almost anything else. And I believe in magic or want to. I want flying saucers to be true, and I want life to exist on Mars, and I dream of a heaven where old friends meet and old enemies embrace one another and weep.* [20]

So, if Keller and Buechner can believe in reunion and get away with it, so can I.

Some people zealously guard their minds, lest a memory of a friend dart onto center stage and demand, "Now what about me?" It takes a lot of energy to keep the memories at bay. And it's impoverishing, according to Amy Dean who, from experience, encourages us to be courageous in summoning the memory of friends:

> *Didn't the person you lost make you laugh? Didn't this person make you smile and feel joy in your heart whenever your eyes met, your voices mingled, and your hands touched?*

> *These are the things you can recall today—the good memories, the fun times, the shared experiences, and the things that made tears of laughter run from your eyes.*

> *Today, take out a scrapbook or photo album and remember with a light heart, the one you lost. Imagine him or her sitting next to you as you flip through the pages together and relive the wonderful moments you shared together.*

*Today I'll speak to the one I lost as if he or she were right beside me.
I'll say, "Do you remember . . . ?" as I talk about a time that will always
bring me joy whenever I think of it.*

—*Amy Dean* [21]

---

*I could not conceive of old age without the many friends I conjure
up from a section of my brain. Engraved in my memory are the thousands of God's creatures I have met in my long life, saints and sinners,
popes and commissars, the possessed and the disposed, the whole and
the injured. I see faces that cling to me, faces I garnered on journeys
around the world. These vast numbers of faces, gathered day and night,
are kept alive in my memory by the fire of a compassion and a love
for drama and humor, tragedy and irony, which I learned long ago.*

—*Fritz Eichenberg* [22]

---

*I have kept everybody's birth date and everybody's death date.
I reflect on those days, and sometimes I just sit in my office for a bit and
think about that person, or I go out for a walk at lunch. Other times I've
gone away for a weekend if it was someone who was particularly close
and reflected on that person.*

*Or I've done something that we had done or shared together. For
example, one friend used to go canoeing with me up north. So, on
occasion I've gone canoeing in that locale by myself to remember.
There are different ways of keeping the person's memory alive, and
they remain with me in thought.*

—*Paul Rapsey* [23]

Remembering can be as simple as noting the anniversaries of
the death, the birthdays one notes but ignores. The calendar has a
way of getting our soul's attention:

The holiest of all holidays are those
Kept by ourselves in silence and apart;
The secret anniversaries of the heart.

—Henry Wadsworth Longfellow [24]

We may fear we will forget something that we desperately want to remember about our friend. We are afraid we will not be able to recall a certain look, or habit, or action—something the person said, or the way it was said. Yet, when we try to hold on to pieces of our memory too tightly, we squeeze them away.

It is better for us to help our memories live. We can do this by recording on tape, or in writing, the things our loved one said, the way he or she looked or acted. We may record our special moments, the times we most enjoyed together. We may assemble notes, photographs, letters, and clippings in one central place so that we will have a tangible memory bank that we can visit any time we wish. We can also invite others who know our loved one to contribute their special memories and observations.

—Carol Staudacher [25]

Sometimes we remember our friends by remembering the great causes and issues that captured their hearts:

The person who had lived for something beyond herself, her political convictions, a special enterprise or a cause—always leaves the living with something more uplifting to do than weep. I can't bring back my dear friend Andrea, for example, who died of cancer last spring at the age of 48, but I can try to make the things she cared about keep going. In the words of my favorite Holly Near song, "It could have been me, but instead it was you. So I'll keep doing the work you were doing as if I were two."

—Barbara Ehrenreich [26]

A contribution to any worthwhile charity is a fitting memorial
to the memory of the deceased.

—*Earl Grollman* [27]

But it is especially meaningful to give to the deceased's favorite charity, on the anniversary of the death, with a note explaining the contribution. Often, our remembrances of a friend are focused on key events, experiences, or encounters that we describe as "the one that sticks out in my mind." Indeed, much of the emotional business, appropriately at a funeral ritual, is the telling—and retelling for late arrivals—and hearing of those key memories, some of which elicit a "That reminds me of the time she . . ." The reality is that our memories become a primer for the memories of others and are, therefore, necessary.

Charles Sheldon Whitehouse, former ambassador to Laos and Thailand, asked how he would remember his friend Jacqueline Kennedy Onassis reminisced:

I remember fox hunting with her in a downpour. "Don't you think we should go on?" I said hopefully. "Oh not yet," she replied, "we're already wet and, who knows, something wonderful might happen." [28]

"Something wonderful" often happens when friends deliberately remember friends. One of America's greatest orators was Everett Dirksen, a senator from Illinois and the Republican minority leader from 1959 until his death in 1969. Within hours of Dirksen's death, the Senate majority leader, Mike Mansfield, had issued a well-worded eulogy of his friend "from across the aisle":

In the first shock of his passing the words do not come. It is too soon. The void has opened suddenly. The emptiness is too complete. It is possible, now, only to sense the loss, to sense it in the profound sorrow which his death brings to us. It was agreed that Dirksen's body should lie in state under the great dome of the Capitol, on the catafalque which had held the body of another Republican from Illinois, Abraham Lincoln.

Mansfield explained that his friend "was a big enough man for it."

Senator Margaret Chase Smith of Maine, who was known for wearing a single red rose, placed a single marigold—the state flower of Illinois—on his Senate desk. Sadly, politics amended the funeral plans. His former Senate jousting partner in the Senate, Lyndon B. Johnson, was asked to deliver the eulogy. But when told he would sit next to President Nixon during the funeral, Johnson declined the opportunity to praise his friend and did not attend the funeral. So, Richard Nixon rose to the occasion in eulogizing his friend and former Senate colleague, saying,

While he never became president, his impact and influence on the nation was greater than most Presidents in our history. . . .

As he could persuade, he could be persuaded. His respect for other points of view lent weight to his own point of view. He was not afraid to change his position if he were persuaded that he had been wrong. That tolerance and sympathy were elements of his character; and that character gained him the affection and esteem of millions of his fellow Americans.

We shall always remember Everett Dirksen in the terms he used to describe his beloved marigolds: hardy, vivid, exuberant, colorful, and uniquely American. [29]

After President John F. Kennedy was assassinated in 1963, his widow, Jackie, went through his possessions, carefully selecting gifts for his trusted associates on the long trek to the White House. To Pierre Sallinger, J.F.K.'s cigar-smoking press secretary and friend, she gave a leather cigar case, one that could hold only two cigars. Jackie Kennedy penned this note:

For Dear Pierre.

I know you carry more cigars than this, but I thought you might like to have this cigar case that belonged to Jack. It comes with all my love and appreciation for all you did to make his day here so unforgettable.

—Jackie. [30]

Some friends prefer not to mention a deceased friend or not to be the first to mention the name. So, friends stand stiffly at some event, engaging in small talk while internally desperately "cracking the whip" and snarling "Back!" at the memories as if they were lions in the cage under the Big Top.

It will be a big mistake to avoid speaking the name cascading through everyone's minds or to avoid naming the loss. It will be a big mistake to pretend that this occasion is unaffected by the loss of our friend. Indeed, the occasion or gathering cannot be the same.

We do ourselves and our friend an injustice by pretending the friend is merely tardy or out of town. Often I have decided to be the first to speak that name. Deliberately. "Wouldn't Denny have loved this . . . ?"

*D*oesn't our friend, now gone
deserve something more than silence
when we gather?
How many times has the "old gang"
gotten together for some reason or
for no particular reason and acted
as if some bylaw exists
to govern the script for the event:
Whatever you do, don't mention her name.
This silence wounds me
because I'm a coward.
If we've silenced and shelved grief for Janet,
the same folks
will shelve their memories of me if,
God forbid, I be the next to go.
Each time we get together I tell myself en route
This . . . is . . . the . . . time!
Break the silence!
Just ad lib from the well-stocked memories
of our friend.

But each time
in the silent rehashing of the event
in the moments before sleep claims me

I realize, that again,
the name went unspoken.
Doesn't our friend, now dead,
deserve more than our silence?

—Harold Ivan Smith

The silence often has an explanation. Some people are already busily engaged in the active business of "replacing" him or her. Any remembering only "complicates" the orderly "white-ing out" of the friend from our minds as well as our memories. After all, "Life goes on . . ." Indeed, this attitude may set the stage for confrontation between friends.

I recognize it in their voices.
"Do you still miss her?"
Still resounds like cannon fire or a
twenty-one gun salute . . .
It ricochets up and down the
canyons of my heart.
Still. The word stings, indites.
There still and the facial expression
which accompanies
their incredulous astonishment
is a gentle rebuke:
as if I am most immature
or in desperate need of a clocked
stretching out on a shrink's couch
for refusing to be "done"
with this particular grief.
"She was only a friend; the way you're
carrying on . . ."

Still.
How shall I answer you?
One still is not enough.

One still cannot begin to capture
the anguish in my heart for this friend
torn from me
and from future memory-making.
Yes, I still . . . with one of those little
mathematical numbers slightly raised
to the nth degree at the end . . .
miss her.

I suspect, given the death
of the friendship,
I will always still miss her.

Is this some type of denial or ego or dysfunction
that I cling to my friend?
Just where am I supposed to start
to look for someone to "replace"
this friend who has died?
I can, with a little effort,
and a few credit cards replace
almost everything in my life
except for this friend.
There may, in time, come another
perhaps one, who will, in many ways
remind me of my friend.
But "replace"?!
Never. Never! NEVER!!!
I will simply have to get used
to this lingering-tinted pain
called friendgrief.

—*Harold Ivan Smith*

There is a Bud-shaped hole in my heart.

—*Harold Ivan Smith*

One way we honor our friends is by sharing the loss with other friends. Some do adopt a "rugged individualism" approach to grief, quietly humming, "I did it my way." But, ironically, the subject of a friend's death can come up out of the blue when talking with someone else:

> *I recall one day high on the Apennine Ridge in Italy when I engaged an old man in conversation. He was seated on a stone wall above a steep valley. I asked for his thoughts. "Everyone with whom I grew up," he answered promptly "is dead."*
>
> *I know what that old man on the Italian hilltop meant when he told me sadly that every friend of his boyhood was dead. My own mind is people now with two or three generations of loved ones who exist only in my memory.*
>
> *I enjoy in these "golden years" thinking back over so many fascinating personalities and so many great events with which I have had contact as a foreign correspondent . . . but I seek also, while I treasure these memories, not to become their prisoner. Life is too magnificent a gift to be spent, even in the golden years, musing about what is no more.*
>
> *—Barrett McGurn* [31]

Sometimes I have been on the giving end in reaching out to someone who is grieving a friend's death. We never know how a greeting card will be received. Perhaps it is the text, or the picture, or the sentiment, or simply the discovery that someone remembered us in our loss of a friend. Cards, notes, and phone calls count—even those left on an answering machine in today's hectic world:

> *What a wonderful, wonderful, wonderful card.*
>
> *You really found the right one—obviously to match your mood and thoughts, and to touch me in a very, very deep place. . . . I really, really needed the words you sent today.*

Today was a day of memories. I'm not sure exactly what brought on the memories, but oh I was missing my special friends today. So when your card arrived, it met a timely need. I needed your kind thoughts of caring and the warmth.

—*Greg DeBourgh* [32]

For the cost of a card and a postage stamp you can make a difference in a grieving person's life. How many times have we missed such an opportunity?

I know one never ceases to remember those whose lives touched ours in a special way. But does there ever come a time when we cease to light a candle and call their name? When does the day, the hour, the moment become no longer need to reflect upon our loss and heaven's gain? My head says the time to stop is now, but my heart says always remember.

—*Nadine Sadler* [33]

The nice thing about putting our sentiments into words is that they can be read and reread. If you distrust your own words, buy or borrow another's but add a note: "Do you remember the time we . . ." An "Oh yes . . ." or "I had forgotten all about that . . ." moment of healing could result.

Alumni magazines unfortunately have obit sections. A quick reading can be a bittersweet experience. I am saddened by the reports of what are clearly premature passings; notices remind me to get on with my professional agenda, lest that be written of me, '74. In skimming the Vanderbilt University alumni magazine, I read that E. Charles Chatfield had received the Warren F. Kuehl Prize for the best book in the past two years in the field of internationalism and peace. Alumni congratulated him on a "job well done." There was more to the story. The book, *An American Ordeal: The Anti-War Movement in the Vietnam Era*, began as the project of Chatfield's friend Charles DeBenedetti. Chatfield, laid aside his own professional priorities, during his friend's battle with cancer, to finish his book. Amazing! In a Toledo hospital room Chatfield assured his dying friend that the book would be completed:

"Your project is a precious child," I said, "and I am conscious that it is your child. My life is like that of a doctor at birth." "Chuck," I said, "you are a good Catholic." He smiled again, genuinely pleased at the thought. "You will understand my meaning if I say that I'll need your continued help." [34]

Charles Chatfield is an academician with a big heart. But that news item left me pondering two questions: Would I do that for a friend? But more troubling: Do I have such a friend as Charles Chatfield in my repertoire? I don't always like the answers to either question.

The death of a friend can re-orient all of our carefully schemed agenda, schedules, and priorities, and leave us like glass shards waiting the broom and dustpan. The death of a friend can leave us staring into our own spiritual darkness. Indeed, grieving for a friend is impacted by what we believe about the "after life." If you only get one spin around the track of life and then are annihilated, the grieving is more devastating. On the other hand, I have chosen deliberately to believe "I will see my friends again." I am encouraged by a poem that Doug Malloch wrote in honor of his friend, Emerson Hough:

Time brings not death, it brings but changes;
I know he rides, but rides afar,
To-day some other planet ranges
And camps to-night upon a star
Where all his other comrades are.

For there were those who rode before him,
As there are these he leaves behind;
Although from us time's changes bore him,
Out there our comrade still will find
The kinship of the comrade mind.

Time brings us change and leaves us fretting;
We weep when every comrade goes—
Perhaps, too much, perhaps forgetting
That over yonder there are those
To whom he comes and whom he knows.

Whatever values we yet may wander,
What sorrows come, what tempest blow,
We have a friend, a friend out yonder,
To greet us when we go—
Out yonder someone that we know.
To all eternity he binds us;
He links the planet and the star;
He rides ahead, the trail he finds us,
And where he is and where we are
Will never seem again so far.

—*Douglas Malloch* [35]

Malloch's imagery of the one "who rides ahead," like the scouts who rode ahead of the wagon train traveling west to California or Oregon, comforts me. The departed are like friends who have arrived at a party early and have already "scouted out" the place, promising, "Wait 'til you see . . ." That has happened so many times here, why wouldn't that happen in the next world? In my work as a speaker, I live on airplanes. I know the experience of scanning the crowd for a familiar face waiting at the end of the jetway. I too know the delight of stepping into a hugged, "Good to see you! Glad you are here!" Eternity may be just that simple.

I can't honestly say what is in my heart. I can only try to say
that nothing is ever lost in life. . . . Our paths cross, and lives are
woven together and each one gives and receives fully and each
one is bound to the others with thanksgiving which can
never be expressed but is the most real thing in life.

—*Stephen F. Bayne Jr.* [36]

The most comforting thought of all would be that I could be
with the people I have loved.

—*Eda LeShan* [37]

After the death of Franklin D. Roosevelt in 1945, a friend sent a note to Eleanor, saying, "They are not dead who live in lives they leave behind. In those whom they have blessed they live a life again." [38] The Quakers were also often known as the "Friends." No wonder. The founder of what is now Pennsylvania said this prayer:

We give back, To you, Oh God,
Those whom you gave to us.
You did not lose them when you gave them to us,
and we do not lose them by their return to you. . . .
Open our eyes to see more clearly, and draw us
closer to you that we may know that we are nearer to our loved ones,
who are with you.

—*William Penn* [39]

———

Oh God
give your glory and your promised future to_____.
We cannot believe
that his/her life has been spent in vain
and that all she/he meant to other people
is lost now that he/she is no longer with us.
We share the faith
by which he/she held unto you to the very end
to you, his/her God and ours,
to you living for us today and every day
forever and ever. Amen.

—*Herb Oosterhuis* [40]

THE RECONCILING

A great deal of what I understand
when I hear or use the word friend
comes not from a bound dictionary
but from an intimacy called friendship
and from the shadings of words
I learned from those I have called friends.

—Harold Ivan Smith

It's amazing how we read something and store a phrase or sentence in our minds. When I read the biography of Martha Berry, founder of Georgia's Berry College, I was moved by her reflections on death:

> *When I am gone, I want you to always think of me as alive—alive beyond your farthest thoughts, and near and loving you, and growing more like God wants me to become.*
>
> *—Martha Berry [1]*

Sometimes grief fuzzes our memory. When the family of my friend Rusty Esposito asked me to say a brief prayer after the internment of his ashes, the Martha Berry quote wouldn't come to mind. That humid summer morning my grief was too fresh to trust spontaneous inspiration. So, I read the words of Henry Scott Holland, at times, and my sight blurred by tears:

> *Death is nothing at all. I have only slipped into the next room. I am I, and you are you. Whatever we were to each other, that we still are. Call me by my old familiar name, speak to me in the easy way which you have always used. Put no difference in your tone, wear no forced air of solemnity or sorrow.*
>
> *Laugh as we always laughed at the little jokes we enjoyed together. Pray, smile, think of me, pray for me. Let my name be ever the household word that it always was, let it be spoken without effect, without the trace of a shadow on it. Life means all that it ever meant. . . . Why should I be out of mind because I am out of sight? I am waiting for you, for an interval, somewhere very near, just around the corner. All is well.*
>
> *—Henry Scott Holland [2]*

Reconciling the loss does not mean "getting over" the death; in reality, emotionally healthy people do not get over or get used to the death. They do not forget their friend. My friend Tony Campolo explained his reconciliation with the death of his friend, Clarence Stevenson:

After that, we would think of Clarence from time to time. And we would miss him. We would cry for Clarence now and then. But our tears would not be like those who have no hope. We Christians can cope with tragedy and sorrow because we know in the midst of what is happening—good and bad, painful or happy, ugly or beautiful—God is at work. [3]

By reconciling, I do not try to squelch thoughts or memories but I welcome them. Alfred Kolatch offered this explanation of reconciliation in *The Jewish Mourner's Book of Why*:

Despite the passage of time and the absence of physical form, I feel their presence, their love, and their influence. The power of their lives is still real, as real as when they were alive. They remain for me a tower of strength, a source of inspiration, and a constant influence for good. The values and lessons they transmitted to me and instilled in me still energize and motivate me. [4]

I have reconciled the deaths of friends by being grateful for having had such friendships. I have come to understand that Death ends life but certainly doesn't rob it of meaning. We all need to remember that in our lives we affect and change the people closest to us. Those changes have a considerable value. For instance, I am not the same person that I would have been had I not met James, Ruth, John, or the many others who have made a lasting impression on me. Some people even think of these changes as some form of immortality. They suggest that people who have died, or who are dying, do live on, in changes they have caused in those who survive them. Having a library or office block named after you cannot make people remember you. But if you've altered the way people think, then some of the meaning of your life will go on after your death.

—*Robert Buckman [5]*

My friends have altered the way I think. By their dying—and the heroism of their battles—caused me to think about the meaning of life in general and my life in particular. They bless me in death even as they blessed me in life. What I know about friendship I learned from them.

*F*riendship resembles
those chemical chains
identified in small print
on product warning labels, such as
tetrahydrozoline hydrochloride.
A substance made up of
tetra
hydro
zoline
hydro
chloride.
Five syllables. Take away any one
and the remainder is a chemical
that has been altered,
now quite unlike the original.
So with friendships:
JohnBudCecilRustyLeonMartinBunnyDennyAnneJohn
DonnieDavidLoisHudsonHaroldIvanSmith
is not the same Harold Ivan Smith
if any of those names be taken away.

     —Harold Ivan Smith

Music has comforted many grievers over the centuries. In churches in eighteenth century England, people sang their grief for friends who had died:

If death my friend and me divide,
thou does not, Lord, my sorrow chide,
or frown my tears to see;
restrained from passionate excess,
thou bidst me mourn in calm distress
for them that rest in thee.

I feel a strong immortal hope,
which bears my mourning spirit up
beneath its mountain load;
redeemed from death, and grief, and pain,
I soon shall find my friend again
within the arms of God.

Pass a few fleeting moments more
and death the blessing shall restore
which death has snatched away;
for me thou will the summons send,
and give me back my parted friend
in that eternal day.

—Charles Wesley [6]

The choice to invest emotionally in a friendship inevitably guarantees an eventual grieving season. Nevertheless . . .

I am richer
by knowing these friends
by having listened to their stories
by having participated in their dramas.

I will not draw up into dark solitude
to prevent losses, future tears.
I will not be stingy with my capacity
to make, to nurture friends.
Long time ago I learned that a person
can never have too many friends.

Yes, I have attended too many funerals
but those have not always been
rituals of sadness.
I have chosen to attend to celebrate
the luxury of friendship
and to remember
a particular friendship.
I am richer, oh, by far,
from those friendships
now momentarily paused.

—Harold Ivan Smith

The good news/bad news scenario could be expressed in these words by Robert Anderson:

Death ends a life:
but it does not end a relationship. [7]

I am reminded of this reality by a framed calligraphy hanging on the wall of a friend's study:

When you look into the night sky
and wonder, Where have they gone?
Place your hands over your heart space
and know they are right there.

—Lon Nungesser [8]

I voice my grief hoping, perhaps, that in my words I can find a slice of meaning waiting my discovery. I voice my grief hoping to find my way into an explanation of the unexplainable, to acquaint myself with the mystery of all this death, realizing that mystery chooses to disrobe only with time.

I voice my grief to express displeasure with the death of a friend like Leon, a college president who had so much more to give; and for Denny, who died at age nineteen with all his life before him; for Bud, my mentor/friend who died while I still needed his wise counsel; for Bob, who posed such challenging faith questions in such tender ways and who published one of my earliest books. The world still needs Leon and Denny and Bud and Bob and all those we named and counted friends. In the writings of two Asian friend-grievers, I found the encouragement to finish this book. Ningkun Wu's powerful memoir, *A Single Tear*, traces his twenty-two year persecution in China, labor camp detention, separation from his family, and the death of friends such as Xiao San and Cha Liangtseng.

Ningkun Wu observed:

> *As I look back and ruminate on the thirty years of my life in*
> *Communist China, the dead and the living who have peopled the*
> *changing landscapes come to live together in my mind.* [9]

Hopefully the "dead and the living who have peopled the changing landscapes" of your life, and who "live together in mind"—your friends—have been summoned to center stage in your heart. Hopefully a whispered "I miss you" has crossed your lips. Nungkun's writing led me to the book *I Myself Am a Woman*, by a university professor, Ding Ling, equally persecuted during the Cultural Revolution. As I sat reading on the floor of Cody Books in Berkeley, Ding's description of her friend Chen Man brought a deep smile to my face and a gasped "Yes. Yes!" for I recognized a fellow friend-griever. Her words are a fitting way to draw our time to a close:

> *Now, whenever there is nothing on my mind, or perhaps when*
> *I need some affection, I recall many people, and Chen Man is one*
> *of them. It is sad at this time all I can do is write down this simple*
> *memoir. However, I hope that by doing so, the people who live*
> *forever in my heart will also live forever in the hearts of others.*
>
> *—Ding Ling* [10]

I hope that you will find creative ways to share the stories of your friendship with those who live forever in your heart. One creative way to remember might be to pray this adaptation of the Jewish Zicorono liveracha:

> *O God, grant us strength as we remember the loss of _____.*
> *May his/her memory be a blessing.* [11]

Cherishing
the
Memory

By reading this book, you have learned something of my friends Rusty, Martin, Alice, John, Anne. Try rereading one of the selections that may have touched you, then take a piece of paper and begin writing what comes into your head. Write! Remember that journal writing is soul work for you.

Tell stories about the deceased or journal about your friend:

- the time I saw my friend speechless . . .

- a favorite Christmas/birthday present from _____

- one thing that _____ loved to do . . .

- the time I saw _____ lose her cool . . .

- the time _____ made me so angry . . .

❧

Give your friendgrief a voice. It deserves your attention just as any other grief you have experienced or will experience.

Remember that your grief counts! "DO" funerals. Some families have been hurt because of the poor attendance. Even the difficult-to-attend funerals can be a way of showing you care by your presence. I'd rather regret going than regret not attending.

Get out the word of the death. Is there someone "out of the loop" who may have moved to another city and does not know of the death? And not everyone reads the obituaries. If you feel awkward, preface this by saying, "You probably already know _____ died . . ." Relationships resemble triangles and you may be the third "side." It is more difficult to deal with the loss, when the feeling "I wish I had known . . ." is countered by "Yeah, well I started to call you but I figured . . ."

Provide flowers for your friend's place of worship, on the birthday or passing day, in honor of your friend. Send a single rose to the family.

Attend the rituals honoring your friend. Your gift of presence will be appreciated.

Remember the family of a friend about three months after a funeral, or as one writer phrased it, "After the flowers have gone." That's when the "thinning" of friends will have taken place and real loss sits in.

Adopt one of your friend's charities. If he or she considered it an important charity, maybe you should become involved. Loss of donors through death hurts great causes; a donation—no matter how small—on the birth date or death date would be a great way to remember your friend.

Plan an informal gathering of friends for the one year anniversary of your friend's death.

Write a note with a specific anecdote to the family. Too many greeting cards are generic. A note with an "I remember the time, she/he" or "one thing that made _____ so special to me was . . ." will be valued by others and may jump start their memories and earn a "Thanks for reminding me of . . ."

Visit the grave or scattering site, and not just on Memorial Day. I sometimes call out, "Hey, Bud!" as I pass the cemetery where my friend Bud is buried. I have also gone by some days and just paused to think a while at his grave or to share a piece of special news. I also take a single rose or carnation during Christmas week to my friend Denny's grave.

Recognize the variety of grief styles. Some of your mutual friends will elect to "get over with it" and get on with their own lives, and will not be as interested in healthily grieving. You may come to the conclusion that your friendship was deeper, more richer than another's. Remember, this is how some have chosen to grieve. Don't be hurt if someone snaps, "I don't want to talk about it!" or changes the subject. Say your friend's name aloud and without apology. When telling a story or talking about a deceased friend, say the name.

Give money to help find a cure for the disease that claimed your friend. Sometimes the designated charity is one preferred by the survivors rather than the deceased; some families deliberately do not designate AIDS-related charities because of the stigma attached. This is a nation with all kinds of foundations working on disease cures. Your contribution helps them move a step closer to a cure. Every extra dollar helps. Perhaps at the time of the loss you were not able to make a contribution to the designated charity. Or in all the emotion of the death, you overlooked it. Contribute now. The organization still needs the money. Or give some time as a volunteer.

Volunteer to be a "grief companion" to someone. When the time is right, drop a note. Say, "I've lost a friend and have experienced a lot in dealing with friendgrief. It has not been easy but I've gotten help from others and from drawing on my own reflection. I'm not an expert but I have learned some things that I would like to share with those who are going through what I've been through. If you ever need to talk, I may not have answers, but I'd be willing to listen."

Make a doxology prayer or poem to give thanks for friendships past and for friendships present. Write a roster of friends, and beside each name write one noteworthy characteristic of that friend or one contribution they made to your life: "_____ introduced me to Thai food."

Compile a scrapbook or collage to highlight your friendship.

Wear something that belonged to your friend. One physician friend wears ties of friend-patients he has lost as a way of remembering them. Many people enjoy wearing the jewelry of a friend. A compliment offers you a chance to mention your friend.

Make provisions in your will for gifts to friends. If you are dying, go ahead and give now so you can share in the giving. Recently, I was with a friend who pointed out some items he wanted me to have. "I'd go ahead and give them to you now," he teased, "but I am not through dusting them, yet."

Remember their family members and friends, particularly those who are having a tough time. Three of my friends are sisters of friends that have died—sisters I had never met until the death of my friends.

Celebrate Memorial Day. We've allowed this day to become just the first day of summer rather than a day to remember those we have loved. Maybe you're going to the lake or to a baseball game; make some time that day to remember your friends and to celebrate the friendship. Offer a toast in their honor.

Continue a tradition initiated by a friend, such as a holiday barbecue, open house, or seasonal party.

Plant or pay for the planting of a tree or bush in the honor of your friend. Monitor the plant's growth over time.

Visit a favorite restaurant. Perhaps initially a full meal will be too bittersweet; so how about dessert and coffee, alone or with another friend?

Look for new projects. When an announcement came across my desk about furnishings for a new branch library, I read with interest about the children's section. Today, in that library, children sit at a table and chairs donated in honor of a friend who was a second grade teacher and budding children's author.

Do something innovative. At a children's museum, I had stars named for two friends. It's wonderful to walk out into the night and know that two of those stars have friends' names.

Watch a video of a movie your friend loved.

Adopt one of your friend's good habits. Greg gives generous tips. When asked why, he noted, "Because Martin [his late friend] did." Martin, as a waiter, had learned the value of tips, so he taught Greg to tip well. Martin also picked up litter on the sidewalks as he walked because he loved his city, so now I do.

Remember the anniversary of the death. A card, letter, phone call to the family or other friends will be appreciated. Many of us settle for remembering "it was about this time of year" rather than the day. Your friend had a specific name and a specific birthday. Why shouldn't you remember the death date as well?

Write a poem about your friend. Make copies and send them to other people who knew your friend.

Explore your grief with a psychologist or counselor. While some people will dismiss or discount your grief, "He was only a friend," do what you need to do to grieve healthily for your friend.

Buy something—like a brick, when a community organization sells things for a fund-raiser—in the name of your friend.

Make your friend's recipes—even though they may never taste quite the same.

Listen to their favorite song; request it on a radio station.

Donate a book or video to a local library in honor of your friend.

Display photos of your friend.

Mention the cause of death in conversations.

Invest in someone's future. My friend Bud Lunn was a strong supporter of a particular seminary. I wanted to honor my friend who had never let me pay for a lunch. So I contacted the seminary and asked what a lectureship would cost. Out of my range, I discovered. But, the president noted, "Your friend always gave money to our scholarship fund. You could start a scholarship in his name." He suggested a minimum amount and then noted it could be financed in installments. Instead of buying a new car, I put the money, month after month, into a scholarship fund named for my friend. Recently, I received a "thank you" letter from the first recipient of that scholarship.

Take someone to the cemetery with you. If you are going to the grave, would you like company? Perhaps someone you know would like to go but does not want to go alone. Or a friend who no longer drives may value an invitation to accompany you.

Toast your friend over a meal with mutual friends, at a holiday, birthday, special occasion, or other celebration.

Go to a favorite place and celebrate the memory of your friend and the privilege of such a friendship. The temptation is to avoid such places, but we need to be reminded of friendships in memory-soaked places.

Check-in by phone or letter with some of your friends' friends. We all know *sorta-friends* through a primary friend. Because of this, it's easy to lose more than one friendship in a death.

Create something of beauty in honor of your friend. The AIDS Quilt has become an incredible repository of memory and a model of healthy remembering. Lots of grievers who have never held a needle have created (with assistance) eloquent creative remembrances for friends. If you can sew, help a friend make a panel. I had a calligrapher take a favorite quotation from a friend and create calligraphy that I gave to my friend's parents and her son. Her words literally danced off the page. The family loved the calligraphies and the remembering behind the gift.

Remember the friends of others who have died. They often will be overlooked in the family-centered formal grieving. A note, card, or phone call will be appreciated especially if you know what it feels like to have your grief overlooked or discounted. Invite them for a meal or coffee and say, "I know you miss your friend . . ."

Donate money to your friend's alma mater.

Name a child after your friend.

Read a friend's favorite book.

Plan a P.D.R. (a post death ritual), such as a gathering, a story-telling, or party to be held weeks or months after the funeral that focuses on the grief of the friends of the deceased.

Be alert to the stigmatized deaths. Some people are tempted to jettison friends who died under strange circumstances. Some may also be afraid to fully disclose the cause of death.

When you want to say, "_____ would have loved this," go ahead and say it—even if only to yourself.

Give yourself time to grieve. All of this about "stages of grief" is just a helpful theory. Grief is an unique as your fingerprints. To paraphrase Frank Sinatra, "Do it your way."

Pray for the dead. Historically, the mainline churches have prayers for the deceased. This is a way of allowing the grieving to verbalize the losses. Sadly, in too many congregations the last time a name is spoken is at the funeral or memorial service.

Offer to assist with chores tied to settling the estate of your friend. You honor your friend by making the task a little easier.

Mention the death of your friend in your letters to others.

Honor the life lessons you learned from your friend.

THE NAMING
of
NAMES

The following ritual is called the "Naming of Names." It is a gathering of grievers and can be used in place of or in addition to a traditional funeral or memorial service.

Notes on the Ritual

One unlighted candle should be on the altar in a church (table in other settings, or around a dining room table if part of a meal) for each friend being remembered. As the name is read the people remembering that friend come up, take a candle and light it from the burning candle, pause for a moment of personal reflection, then return to their seat. If the Naming is for one friend, you can have one candle for each person who gives witness to the life of the friend. Ask participants to bring pictures of their friend for display.

At the close of the Naming, the candles may be given to the participants. If a large number of people participate, write the remembered name on a small card and place by the candle so participants can identify a particular candle to light and to keep.

If a minister participates, she or he could offer a brief meditation or prayer. Or this could be offered by a participant using or adapting one of the prayers in this book. The program can be duplicated in an attractive format as a way of remembering the gathering. Prepare extra copies to share with family or other friends who could not participate. Include some special quotations in the program.

- Assign participants to read passages. Or ask participants to bring favorite quotes of their friend.

- Favorite music of the friend can be sung or played at the Naming. The leaders will find it helpful to know the selections for the best placement in the ritual.

- Refreshments after the Naming will be welcomed. You might have a meal or potluck together as part of the Naming. If so, prepare a favorite recipe of your friend's. Toast your friend.

- Expect that some participants will want to linger for more informal reminiscing and story-telling.

- Videotape the Naming for future reference and to share with friends who could not attend.

The Naming of Names

Welcoming

Leader: We have come to this Naming to give witness to the life of our friend [pause for participants to voice the name] _____ or friends _____.

All: May _____'s memory to us be a blessing.

The Leader: Let us pray:

You have blessed us, O God, with the gift of friendship. Thank you for friends who have enriched our lives. We pause this day/night to give witness to the life of our friend(s) _____ [pause for the names to be called out] who loved us and whom we loved. Our friend shared our joys, listened to our stories, participated in our celebrations, wept with us in our woundedness, and was there for us when we needed [him/her/them]. As we remember _____'s life give us faith to sense in death the promise of eternal life. Give us the courage to take advantage of opportunities to remember well such a friend/such friends. Amen.

Shared Reading: Psalm 23

Leader: The Lord is my shepherd.

The Gathering: I shall lack nothing.

Leader: He makes me lie down in green pastures;

The Gathering: He leads me beside quiet waters.

All: He restores my soul;

Leader: He guides me in the paths of righteousness for his name's sake. Even though I walk through the valley of the shadow of death.

Gathering: I will fear no evil; for you are with me;

Leader: You prepare a table before me

Gathering: in the presence of my enemies.

Leader: You anoint my head with oil;

Gathering: my cup overflows.

Leader: Surely goodness and love will follow me all the the days of my life,

Gathering: And I will dwell in the house of the Lord

All: forever.

Readings: *John 14:1-7, John 11:25-26, or Job 19:25-27 may be read by either the leader or by participants. Or a friend's favorite Scripture can be used. If desired, a sermon or brief reflection on the Scripture may follow the reading of the gospel.*

Intercessions

Leader: For _____, our friend who has died, let us pray to the Lord who said, "I am the resurrection and the life."

Gathering: Hear us, Lord.

Leader: Lord, you consoled Mary and Martha in their distress when your friend Lazarus died; draw near to us who in this place remember our friend.

Gathering: Hear us, Lord.

Leader: Lord, you wept publicly and openly at the grave of Lazarus, comfort us in our loss.

Gathering: Hear us Lord.

Leader: Lord, you raise the dead to life eternal; give our friend or _____ who has finished the course in faith joyous eternal life.

Leader: Hear us Lord.

Gathering: Lord, your compassion is without measure. You know our feeling of loss with _____'s death. We are aware of the uncertainty of human life; remind us of the preciousness of friends with whom we share our lives.

Gathering: Hear us, Lord.

The Calling of the Names:

As the name of each friend is read, you are invited to come light a candle in their honor. After lighting the candle, you may pause for a moment of private reflection or you may return to your seat. (Or participants can disclose a characteristic of the friend or a word that captures the friend's personality.)

In a gathering where several friends are being named, each name to be honored appears in left column of the program, the name of the person remembering appears in the right column. For example:

David Alan Morrison   *Remembered by Elizabeth Kelley*

If only one friend is being named, each person who shares with the group lights a candle. After you light the candle, turn to the group and say, "I would like to [give witness to/celebrate] the life of my friend, _____." Share a particular incident, memory or characteristic of your friend with the group.

You may want to write out your words—someone may be moved by your words and want a copy. In spontaneous sharing, it's easy to forget something you wanted to say; writing it down is a reminder.

You may want to use a quotation from the book as a way of introducing your sharing. If the Naming is in honor of one friend, you could ask participants to bring a magazine picture that reminds of a shared experience with the friend. The speaker may begin, "This picture reminds me of the time we . . ." Then the speaker glues the picture to a large sheet of posterboard. Thus, a collective collage is done during the Naming.

Closing Prayer:

The group stands, joins hands, and makes a circle for the closing prayer: spontaneous from one participant or the prayer below.

> **Leader:** Creator of all, we pray to you for our friends(s) we know and love, but can no longer see. By the sharing of our memories, by our laughter, by our tears, by our paused silences, and by the lighting of these candles, we have been reminded of the influence of this friend and we have been reminded of how much we miss our friends. Grant our friend rest eternal and let light perpetual shine upon [her/him].

> *Or say:*

> In this hour of remembrance, I pray that these feelings of gratefulness never recede as I now

recall those friends who were closest and dearest to me. May their souls ever be linked with my soul, and may they rest in peace. [1]

Or say this prayer in unison:

O God, grant us strength as we mourn the loss of _____. We will always have cherished memories of him/her. Bless us with light and peace. May _____'s memory continue to serve as a blessing and an inspiration to all who know and loved him/her. [2]

The Blessing:

All: May their memory to us be a blessing!

Or recite this ancient Irish prayer in unison:

God be good to their souls
God rest them
God rest their souls
God have mercy on them. [3]

NOTES

Dedication

1. Susan Ford Wiltshire. *Seasons of Grief and Grace*. Nashville: Vanderbilt University Press, 1994, 145.

Introduction

1. Helen Fitzgerald. *The Mourning Book*. New York: Simon and Schuster, 1994, 138.
2. "Births and Deaths in the U.S." *The World Almanac and Book of Facts*. Mahwah, N.J.: Funk and Wagnals, 1995.
3. Lillian Rubin. *Intimate Strangers: Men and Women Together*. New York: Harper and Row, 1983, 129.
4. Deena Metzer, quoted in Letty Cottin Pogrebin. *Among Friends*. New York: McGraw-Hill, 1987, 106.
5. Marcia and David Kaplan. *Friends: Lovable, Livable, Laughable Lines*. No city of publication: David Kaplan and Marcia Kaplan, 1984, no pagination.
6. Lauren Bacall. *Now*. New York: Knopf, 1994, 152.
7. Fred Sklar. "Grief as a Family Affair: Property Rights, Grief Rights, and the Exclusion of Close Friends as Survivors." *Omega*, 1991-1992, 109.
8. Carolyn H. Oehler. "Scarritt Loses Two Long-Time Friends." *The Arches*. Nashville: Scarritt-Bennett Center, Vol. 6 (3): Summer 1995, 8.
9. Mary-Ellen Siegel. "What About Me?" Chapter 2 in *Unrecognized and Unsanctioned Grief*. Eds. Vanderlyn R. Pine, Otto S. Magnolis, Kenneth Doka, et. al. Springfield, Ill.: Charles C. Thomas, 1993, 13.
10. Molly Porter to Harold Ivan Smith, personal correspondence.
11. Amy E. Dean. *Proud to Be*. New York: Bantam, 1994, June 6.
12. Laurence Binyon, "For the Fallen." *The War Poets*. Ed. Robert Giddings. New York: Orion Books, 1988, 16-17.
13. Peter Cameron. *The Weekend*. New York: Plume/Penguin, 1994, 216-217.
14. Pogrebin, 106.
15. Vincent Lipe to Harold Ivan Smith, personal correspondence, December 14, 1994.

The Passing

1. Gladiola Montana. *Never Ask A Man The Size of His Spread.* Salt Lake City: Gibbs-Smith, 1993, 102.

2. Seneca, in *A Treasury of Friendships.* Ed. Ralph I. Woods. New York: David McKay, 1957, 227.

3. Henri J. Nouwen. *Our Greatest Gift: A Meditation on Dying and Caring.* San Francisco: Harper San Francisco, 1994, 63.

4. Jeanette R. Folta and Edith S. Deck. "Grief, the Funeral and the Friend," *Acute Grief and the Funeral.* Eds.Vanderlyn R. Pine, David Peretz, and A. H. Kushner. Springfield, Ill.: Charles C. Thomas, 1976, 170.

5. Robert Buckman. *I Don't Know What to Say.* Boston: Little, Brown, 1989, 72-73.

6. Ibid., 18.

7. Nina Herrmann Donnelley. *I Don't Know What to Say.* New York: Ballentine, 1987, 160.

8. Montana, 63.

9. Edgar Allen Imhoff. *Always of Home: A Southern Illinois Childhood.* Carbondale, Ill.: Southern Illinois University Press, 1993, 137-138.

10. Henry David Thoreau, quoted in *Book of Quotations.* Ed. Franklin Pierce Adams. New York: Funk and Wagnals, 1952, 366.

11. James Bresnahan. "Catholic Spirituality and Medical Interventions in Dying." *America,* June 29, 1991, 675.

12. Stephen F. Morin and Walter F. Batchelor. "Responding to the Psychological Crisis of AIDS." *Health Reports,* January/February 1984, 7.

13. Ralph David Abernathy. *And the Walls Came Tumbling Down.* New York: Harper and Row, 1989, 442-444.

14. Renita J. Weems. *I Asked for Intimacy.* San Diego: LuraMedia, 1993, 105.

15. Fawn M. Brodie. *Thomas Jefferson: An Intimate History.* New York: Norton, 1974, 452, 468; Page Smith. *John Adams,* Vol. 2: 1784-1826. Garden City: Doubleday, 1962, 1122, 1137.

16. George Seaver. *David Livingstone: His Life and Letters.* New York: Harper and Brothers, 1957, 595-597.

17. North Callahan. *George Washington: Soldier and Man.* New York: Morrow, 1972, 277.

18. Stephen E. Ambrose. *Nixon: Ruin and Recovery 1973-1990,* Vol. 3. New York: Simon and Schuster, 1991, 514-515.

19. Michael S. Piazza. *Holy Homosexuals: The Truth About Being Gay or Lesbian and Christian*. Dallas: Sources of Hope Publishing House, 1994, 182.

20. Joseph P. Lash. *Eleanor: The Years Alone*. New York: Norton, 1972, 329.

21. Ibid., 332.

22. Nelson Mandela. *Long Walk to Freedom: The Autobiography of Nelson Mandela*. Boston: Little, Brown, 1994, 530-531.

23. Jeannie M. Hittle. "Dealing with Death: Grieving Together." *American Journal of Nursing*, July 1995, 55.

24. Rebecca Laird. "In A Woman's Voice: Facing Fear." *Herald of Holiness*, October 1991, 42.

25. Doris Grumbach, *Coming Into the End Zone: A Memoir*. New York: Norton, 1991, 56-57.

26. Thomas H. Johnson. *Emily Dickinson: An Interpretative Biography*. Cambridge, Mass.: Belknap Press of Harvard University, 1955, 205.

27. Dorothy Freeman. *Always Rachel: The Letters of Rachel Carson and Dorothy Freeman, 1952-1964*. Ed. Martha Freeman. Boston: Beacon Press, 1995, 541.

28. Ted Menten. *After Goodbye*. Philadelphia: Running Free Press, 1994, 11.

29. Anonymous. "Seeds of Kindness," in *Poems That Touch the Heart*. Compiled by A. L. Alexander. Garden City: Doubleday, 1956, 115.

30. Nouwen, 45-46.

31. Buckman, 25.

32. Chris Glasser. *The Word Is Out*. San Francisco: Harper San Francisco, 1994, January 27.

33. Grumbach, 121-122.

34. Beatrice Ash. *A Time to Live, A Time to Die*. Minneapolis: Augsburg, 1993, 36-37.

35. Joe Brown, ed. *A Promise to Remember: The Names Project: Book of Letters*. New York: Avon, 1992, 129.

36. Virginia Deyo, quoted in Neal Hutchins. *Voices That Care*. Los Angeles: Lowell House, 1992, 272-273.

37. Donnelley, 162.

38. Carmen L. Cartagirone. *Friendship as Sacrament*. New York: Abba House, 1988, 27.

39. Anna Cummins, quoted in *Words and Wisdom: More Good Advice*. Ed. William Safire and Leonard Safir. New York: Simon and Schuster, 1989, 21-22.

40. Hawley Lincoln. "Grief and the Funeral Director." Chapter 10 in *Unrecognized and Unsanctioned Grief*, 158-160.
41. Arnold E. Beisser. *The Only Gift: Thoughts on The Meaning of Friends and Friendship*. New York: Doubleday, 1991, 8.
42. *The Book of Common Prayer*. New York: Seabury, 1979, 481.
43. Joan Bel Geddes. *Are You Listening God?* Notre Dame, Ind.: Ava Maria Press, 1994, 112.

The Burying

1. Fenton Jones. "The Weight of Memory." *San Francisco Focus* 41: January 1994, 53.
2. Betty Friedan. *The Fountain of Age*. New York: Simon and Schuster, 1993, 544-545.
3. Calvin Trillin. *Remembering Denny*. New York: Warner, 1993, 19-21.
4. Elizabeth Stuart, ed. *Daring to Speak Love's Name: A Gay and Lesbian Prayer Book*. London: Hamish Hamilton, 1991, 130.
5. Mandela, 531.
6. Pogrenin, 107.
7. C. W. Gusewelle. "George Burg Bossed Staff with Fairness, Humor, Generosity." *Kansas City Star*, March 6, 1995, B-1.
8. *The Kansas City Star*, November 7, 1995.
9. Frederick Buechner. *Whistling in the Dark: An ABC Theologized*. San Francisco: Harper and Row, 1988, 51.
10. Barbara Blake. "The Lavender Quill." *Current News*, September 1, 1994, 28.
11. George Gurley. "A Not So Gentle Reminder." *Kansas City Star*, October 26, 1992, C-1.
12. Trillin, 27-29.
13. Imahoff, 144-145.
14. Robert E. Kavanaugh. *Facing Death*. Los Angeles: Nash, 1972, 15-16.
15. Sallie Bingham. *Passion and Prejudice: A Family Memoir*. New York: Knopf, 1989, 359.
16. Bill Huebsch with David Patterson. *A Radical Guide for Catholics*. Mystic, Conn.: Twenty-third Publications, 1992, 157-159.
17. Joseph R. Bankoff. "A Tribute: A Man Who Sold You on Yourself." *The Atlanta Constitution*, November 13, 1994, D9.

18. J. K. Alwood. "Unclouded Day," quoted in Wendell Berry. *Watch with Me and Other Stories*. San Francisco: Pantheon Books, 1994, 206.

19. Carl Solberg. *Hubert Humphrey: A Biography*. New York: Norton, 1984, 456.

20. Jimmy Carter. *Keeping Faith: Memoirs of a President*. New York: Bantam, 1982, 269, 271, 272.

21. *Closest Companion: The Unknown Story of the Intimate Friendship Between Franklin Roosevelt and Margaret Suckley*. Ed. Geoffrey C. Ward. Boston: Houghton-Mifflin, 1995, 420-422.

22. Howard Richman. "Many Blades Gather for Colman Service." *Kansas City Star*, April 8, 1994, D-1, 8.

23. Warren Rogers. *When I Think of Bobby: A Personal Memoir of the Kennedy Years*. New York: Harper Collins, 1993, 184-185.

24. *Closest Companion*, 421-422.

25. Phyllis Theroux. "The Life and Death of a Mayor." *The Washington Post*, October 21, 1990, C5.

26. Ronald O. Valdiserri. *Gardening in Clay: Reflections on AIDS*. Ithica, N.Y.: Cornell University Press, 1994, 75.

27. Eugenia Price. *Getting Through the Night*. Large print edition. New York: Walker and Company, 1982, 19.

28. Abernathy, 464.

29. Ron DelBene, Mary Montgomery, and Herb Montgomery. *From the Heart*. Nashville: Upper Room Books, 1991, 29-30.

30. David McCullough. *Truman*. New York: Simon and Schuster, 1992, 985.

31. Lester David and Irene David. *Bobby Kennedy: The Making of a Folk Hero*. New York: Dodd, Mead, 1986, 317-318.

32. Thomas H. Johnson. *Emily Dickinson: An Interpretative Biography*. Cambridge, Mass.: Belknap Press of Harvard University Press, 1955, 205.

33. "Gerald," quoted in Francis van den Boom. "Point of View: AIDS in the Family: A Personal Reflection." *AIDS Patient Care*, December 5, 1991, 273.

34. Betty J. Carmack. "Balancing Engagement/Detachment in AIDS-related Multiple Loss." *Image*, Spring 1992, 12.

35. Marilyn E. Gootman. *When A Friend Dies*. Minneapolis: Free Spirit, 1994, 6.

36. Ibid., 51.

37. The phrase "through the narrow gate and across the wide, deep river" is found in a prayer by Jim Cotter in *Sebastian Sandys*, 100.

38. *The Book of Common Prayer*, 465.

39. Kerry M. Olitzky and Ronald H. Isaacs. *The How-To Handbook for Jewish Living*. Hoboken, N.J.: KTAV Publishing, 1993, 99.

The Mourning

1. Madeleine L'Engle. *Two Part Invention*. New York: Farrar, Straus, and Giroux, 1988, 228.

2. Donnelley, 170.

3. Ibid., 171-172.

4. Nathan Schachner. *Alexander Hamilton*. New York: A. S. Barnes, 1946, 388.

5. Gootman, 26.

6. Carla Cantor. "Woman to Woman: How Could I Forgive Myself." *Ladies Home Journal*, May 1994, 108-110.

7. Hope Edelman, quoted in Nancy Caldwell Sorel. "Grief Has No Beginning, Middle, or End." *New York Times Book Magazine* (May 15, 1994, 23), reviewing *Motherless Daughters: The Legacy of Loss*.

8. Carol Staudacher. *A Time to Grieve*. San Francisco: Harper San Francisco, 1994, 2.

9. Joseph P. Lash. *Eleanor: The Years Alone*. New York: Bantam, 1972, 237.

10. Bernard Asbell, ed. *Mother and Daughter: The Letters of Eleanor and Anna Roosevelt*. New York: Coward, McCann and Geoghegan, 1982, 299.

11. Edgar N. Jackson. *Understanding Grief*. Nashville: Abingdon, 1957, 143.

12. Alan Zweibel. *Bunny Bunny: Gilda Radner, A Sort of Love Story*. New York: Villard, 1994, 189.

13. Margot Hover. *Caring for Yourself When Caring for Others*. Mystic, Conn.: Twenty-third Publications, 1993, 9-11.

14. Price, 66-67.

15. Jonathan Lazear, 50.

16. Patrick J. Farmer. "Bereavement Counseling." *Journal of Pastoral Care*, Fall/Winter, 1980, 32.

17. Frederick Buechner. *Telling the Truth: The Gospel as Tragedy, Comedy, and Fairy Tale*. San Francisco: Harper and Row, 1977, 36-37.

18. Manning, 60.

19. Ibid., 65.

20. Louis F. Kavar. *Living With Loss*. Gaithersburg, M.D.: Chi Rio Press, 1991, 12.

21. L'Engle, 229.

22. Geddes, 113.

23. Rufus Coleman. "Escaping, Perhaps to Return." *Dallas Morning News*, July 22, 1994, C-1.

24. Ishbell Ross. *Angel of the Battlefield: The Life of Clara Barton*. New York: Harper and Brothers, 1956, 260.

25. Ken Hoover and Katy Butler. "2 San Francisco Marches Go Peacefully." *San Francisco Chronicle*, May 18, 1992, A15.

26. Franklin Abbott, quoted in William A. Henry III. "An Identity Forged in Flames." *Time*, August 3, 1992, 36.

27. Folta and Deck, 239.

28. Hannah Sluss. "Silence Can Hurt." *Parade Magazine*, April 14, 1991, 18.

29. John Donne, quoted in *Bartlett's Familiar Quotations*. Ed. Emily Morison Beck. Boston: Little, Brown, 1980, 254:22.

30. Lord Byron, quoted in *Words and Wisdom: More Good Advice*. Ed. William Safire and Leonard Safir. New York: Simon and Schuster, 1989, 151.

31. Margaret Truman. *Bess W. Truman*. New York: Macmillan, 1986, 432.

32. Nessa Rapport. *A Woman's Book of Grieving*. New York: Morrow, 1994, 15.

33. Lon Nungesser. *Axioms for Survivors*. Expanded edition. San Francisco: Harper San Francisco, 1992, 94.

34. Debra Jarvis. *HIV Positive*. Oxford: Lyon, 1992, 44.

35. Grumbach, 57.

36. James P. Bell. "AIDS and the Hidden Epidemic of Grief." *The American Journal of Hospice Care*, May/June 1988, 30.

37. "Cicero," quoted in Brian Patrick McGuire. *Friendship and Community: The Monastic Experience*, 350-1250. Cistercian Studies Series, Kalamazoo, Mich.: Cistercian Publications, 1988, xxxiv.

38. Maya Angelou. *Wouldn't Take Nothing for My Journey Now*. New York: Random House, 1994, 47-48.

39. Arlene Shannon. "In Memory of Ron Phillips." *St. Luke's Singles* newsletter, St. Luke's United Methodist Church. Indianapolis, Ind. (July 1994), 14, 17.

40. Desmond Tutu. *The Rainbow People of God*. Ed. John Allen. New York: Doubleday, 1994, 16.

41. Henri J. Nouwen. *Life of the Beloved*. New York: Crossroad, 1992, 93.

42. Angelou, 48-49.

43. C. S. Lewis. *Poems.* Ed. Walter Hooper. San Diego: Harcourt, Brace, and Jovanovich, 1964, 118.
44. Paul Carnes, quoted in Elizabeth Stuart, 141.
45. Phillip Yancey. "The Day I'll Get My Friends Back." *Christianity Today,* April 3, 1995, 120.
46. Leonard M. Zunin and Hilary Stanton Zunin. *The Art of Condolence.* New York: Harper Collins, 1991, 199.
47. Angelou, 48.
48. Nungesser, 105.
49. Kathryn Casey. "I'm a Survivor." *Ladies Home Journal,* March 1993, 210.
50. Jane Whitney. *Abigail Adams.* Boston: Little, Brown, 1947, 324.
51. Staudacher, 7.
52. Bertha Simos. *A Time to Grieve.* New York: Family Services Association of America, 1979, 233.
53. Hover, 10.
54. Mandela, 542.
55. Ted Menten, 83.
56. Lazear, 21.
57. Farmer, 29.
58. Anna Quindlen. "Death Carves a Chasm of Loss Deep in the Center of Life." *Kansas City Star,* May 5, 1994, C-5.
59. "Passages." *The Seattle Times,* December 20, 1992, A16.
60. Quindlen, C-5.
61. Angelou, 47.
62. "A Lost War." *Time,* April 24, 1995, 22.
63. Tobias Wolff. "After the Crusade." *Time,* April 24, 1995, 48.
64. Wolff, 48.
65. Dean, April 10.
66. *The Book of Common Prayer,* 505.

The Remembering

1. Thomas Gunn. *The Man With the Night Sweats.* New York: Farrar, Straus, Giroux, 1992, 76.
2. Peter S. Hawkins, "Naming Names: The Art of Memory and the NAMES Project AIDS Memorial Quilt." *Critical Inquiry,* Summer, 1993, 752, cited

in Rob Baker, *The Art of AIDS: From Stigma to Conscience*. New York: Continuum, 1994, 132.

3. Barbara Howes. "A Letter from the Carribean," from *In The Midst of Winter*. Ed. Mary Jane Moffat. New York: Vintage, 1992, 194-195.

4. Menten, 51.

5. Henry David Thoreau, quoted in *A Rumor of Angels: Quotations for Living, Dying, and Letting Go*. Eds. Gail Perry and Jill Perry. New York: Macmillian, 1989, 54.

6. Seneca, quoted in *Book of Quotations*, 364.

7. John Carmody. *Toward A Male Spirituality*. Mystic, Conn.: Twenty-third Publications, 1990, 92.

8. Price, 67.

9. Jeff Black, in conversation with Harold Ivan Smith.

10. François Mauriac, quoted in Perry and Perry, 53.

11. Larry McMurtry. *The Late Child*. New York: Simon and Schuster, 1995, 267.

12. Yancey, 120.

13. Valdiserri, 75.

14. William Nichols. "A Letter to a Friend," in *The Courage to Grow Old*. Ed. Phillip L. Berman. New York: Ballentine, 1989, 233.

15. Nouwen, *Our Greatest Gift*, 71.

16. Joyce Rupp. *Praying Our Goodbyes*. Notre Dame, Ind.: Ava Maria Press, 1988, 93.

17. *Writings on the Wall: The Vietnam Veterans Memorial*. Ed. Jim Scruggs. Washington, D.C.: The Vietnam Veterans Memorial Fund, 1994, 46-47.

18. Doris Grumbach. *Extra Innings: A Memoir.* New York: Norton, 1994, 297.

19. Joseph P. Lash. *Helen and Teacher*. New York: Delacorte, 1990, 786.

20. Frederick Buechner. *Alphabet of Grace*. New York: Harper and Row, 1970, 41-42.

21. Dean, March 3.

22. Fritz Eichenberg. "Image Making as Immortality," in *The Courage to Grow Old*. Ed. Phillip R. Berman. New York: Ballentine, 1989, 281.

23. Paul Rapsey, quoted in Katherine Fair Donnelley. *Recovering from the Loss of a Loved One to AIDS*. New York: St. Martin's Press, 1994, 160.

24. Henry Wadsworth Longfellow. "Holidays," in *Poems That Touch the Heart*. Compiled by A. L. Alexander. Garden City: Doubleday, 1956, 203.

25. Staudacher, 212.

26. Barbara Ehrenreich. "Coming of Age." *Lear's*, September 1993, 46.
27. Earl Grollman, ed. *Concerning Death: A Practical Guide for the Living*. Boston: Beacon Press, 1974, 128.
28. "Remembering Jackie: The People Whose Lives She Touched Talk to Us." *Town and Country,* July 1994, 63.
29. Neil MacNeil. *Dirksen: Portraits of a Public Man*. New York: World, 1970, 388, 389-390.
30. "Remembering Jackie," 62.
31. Barrett McGurn. "Exulting in What Remains," in Berman, 119, 121.
32. Greg DeBourgh to Harold Ivan Smith, personal correspondence, February 17, 1995.
33. Nadine Sadler to Harold Ivan Smith, personal correspondence, February 6, 1995.
34. Charles Chatfield. *An American Ordeal: The Antiwar Movement of the Vietnam Era*. Syracuse, N.Y.: Syracuse University Press, 1990, xi.
35. Douglas Malloch. "A Comrade Rides Ahead," in *The Home Book of Modern Verse*. Ed. Burton Egbert Stevenson. New York: Henry Holt, 1950, 100-101.
36. Stephen F. Byrne Jr. Greeting card published by Saint Mark's Cathedral, Seattle.
37. Edna LeShan. *Oh, To Be 50 Again!* New York: Times Books, 1986, 338.
38. Doris Kearns Goodwin. *No Ordinary Time*. New York: Simon and Schuster, 1984, 633.
39. William Penn, quoted in Perry and Perry, 59.
40. Herb Oosterhuis. *Your Word Is Near*. New York: Paulist Press, 1968, np, cited in Edward J. Siedlecki. *Prayers of Those Who Mourn*. Chicago: Liturgical Training Publications, 1982, 13.

The Reconciling

1. Joyce Blackburn. *Martha Berry: Little Woman With A Big Dream*. Philadelphia: Lippincott, 1968, 158.
2. Henry Scott Holland, quoted in Elizabeth Stuart, 141-142.
3. Tony Campolo. *The Kingdom of God Is A Party*. Dallas: Word, 1990, 130.
4. Alfred Kolatch. *The Jewish Mourner's Book of Why*. Middle Village, N.Y.: Jonathan David Publishers, 1993, 348.
5. Buckman, 11.

6. Charles Wesley, quoted in Richard Foster, *Prayers From the Heart*. San Francisco: Harper San Francisco, 1994, 91.
7. Robert Anderson, quoted in Dean, March 3.
8. Nungesser, 125.
9. Ningkun Wu, with Yikai Li. *A Single Tear*. Boston: Little, Brown, 1993, 355.
10. *I Myself Am A Woman: Selected Writings of Ding Ling*. Ed. Tani E. Barlow, with Gary J. Bjorge. Trans. Jean James. Boston: Beacon, 1989, 328.
11. Olitzky and Isaacs, 97.

The Naming of Names

1. Kolatch, 348.
2. Olitzky and Isaacs, 97.
3. Pat Fairon. *Irish Blessings: Irish Prayers and Blessings*. San Francisco: Chronicle Books, 1993, 43.

Acknowledgements

The publisher gratefully acknowledges the use of excerpts from the following sources. Any omissions are entirely unintentional and will be corrected upon future printings.

The Passing

Our Greatest Gift, by Henri J. M. Nouwen. Copyright © 1994 by Henri J. M. Nouwen. Reprinted by permission of HarperCollins Publishers, Inc.

Unrecognized and Unsanctioned Grief, edited by Vanderlyn R. Pine. Copyright © 1990 Charles C. Thomas. Reprinted by permission of Charles C. Thomas, Springfiled, Ill.

I Don't Know What to Say, by Robert Buckman. Copyright © 1988 by Robert Buckman. Reprinted by permission of Little, Brown and Company.

And the Walls Came Tumbling Down, by Ralph D. Abernathy. Copyright © 1989 by Ralph David Abernathy. Reprinted by permission of Harper-Collins Publishers, Inc.

I Asked for Intimacy, by Renita Weems. Copyright © 1993 LuraMedia. Reprinted by permission of LuraMedia, Inc., San Diego, Calif.

Always, Rachel, edited by Martha Freeman. Copyright © 1995 Martha Freeman. Reprinted by permission of Beacon Press.

The Word Is Out, by Chris R. Glaser. Copyright © 1994 Chris R. Glaser. Reprinted by permission of HarperCollins Publishers, Inc.

Friendship as Sacrament, by Carmen Caltagirone. Copyright © 1988 Alba House, New York. Reprinted by permission.

The Burying

Remembering Denny, by Calvin Trillin. Copright © 1993 Calvin Trillin. Reprinted by permission of Farrar, Straus and Giroux, Inc.